*The author:* Howard Thurman is Dean of the Chapel at Boston University and is Professor of Spiritual Disciplines and Resources in the School of Theology. He was for many years pastor of The Church for the Fellowship of All Peoples in San Francisco. His previous books include DEEP RIVER, THE CREATIVE ENCOUNTER, MEDITATIONS OF THE HEART, DEEP IS THE HUNGER, THE NEGRO SPIRITUAL SPEAKS OF LIFE AND DEATH. (See back panel for description.)

# THE GROWING EDGE

## THE GROWING EDGE

All around us worlds are dying and new worlds are being born;
All around us life is dying and life is being born.
The fruit ripens on the tree;
The roots are silently at work in the darkness of the earth
Against the time when there shall be new leaves, fresh blossoms, green fruit.
Such is the growing edge!
It is the extra breath from the exhausted lung,
The one more thing to try when all else has failed,
The upward reach of life when weariness closes in upon all endeavor.
This is the basis of hope in moments of despair,
The incentive to carry on when times are out of joint
And men have lost their reason; the source of confidence
When worlds crash and dreams whiten into ash.
The birth of a child—life's most dramatic answer to death—
This is the Growing Edge incarnate.
Look well to the growing edge!

# HOWARD THURMAN

# THE GROWING EDGE

HARPER & BROTHERS

To my wife
Who combines the detachment of the critic
with the sensitiveness of the artist
and who makes them serve the commands of the heart

# CONTENTS

vii

# PREFACE

This is a book of sermons. They are transcriptions taken from a tape recorder and carefully edited. Such a procedure is one of the penalties exacted because I do not preach from a written manuscript or notes. The effort has been to retain the quality of the vital spoken word without doing violence to the integrity of the essay. The generous and skilled services of Miss Grace Marrett, a friend who lives in Burlingame, California, provided the critical assistance in this matter that could come only from an inspired and competent devotion.

The attention of the reader is called to the worship pattern in which the sermons appear. Wherever possible there has been included with a particular sermon the meditation-prayer that was used when the sermon was presented. In every instance there is included the quotation which was read as a prolegomenon to the sermon itself. Some of these quotations are taken from material previously written by the author. Wide use has been made of Oswald W. S. McCall's *The Hand of God*, one of the finest worship manuals I have ever read. The readings may or may not bear directly upon the meaning of the sermon. Their primary purpose is to aid the listeners in bringing their minds into focus upon some searching insight and to make available the centered spirits.

For me the sermon is an act of worship in which the preacher exposes his spirit and mind as they seek to reveal the working of the spirit of the living God upon them. It is a searching moment! The atmosphere is one charged with the dynamics of worship and the surrender and commitment which worship inspires.

These sermons were preached as a part of the worship experience of a wide variety of congregations: College, university and preparatory school chapels, Jewish synagogues and Protestant churches. They reveal aspects of my own pilgrimmage without benefit of the magic of the spoken word, the creative pause, and the lifted countenance. For many years, the same prayer precedes each preaching experience—"Search me, O God, and know my heart, try me and know my thoughts. . . ."

One of my professors in homelitics said to our senior class apropos of a student's sermon that had not been well done: "The preacher is never under obligation to preach a great sermon but he is always under obligation to wrestle with a great idea." It is in such a mood that these sermons are published.

My personal gratitude goes to Miss Sydna Altschuler, an undergraduate in the College of Liberal Arts, Boston University, who typed and retyped the manuscript, and to my secretary, Miss Margaret Harding, who rendered the type of service only possible to one who carries the responsibility of the details of an office. As indicated above, the manuscript would not have been possible if I had not been blessed with the co-operation of Miss Grace Marrett.

And what shall I say of my congregations? For twelve years the student-faculty audience in Andrew Rankin Memorial Chapel, Howard University; for nine and one-half years, the challenging cross-section of people who made up the congregation of the Church for the Fellowship of All Peoples, San Francisco; and for the past three years the rare combination of community and university, enriched by men and women of many cultures and many hues who worship on Sunday morning in the Daniel L. Marsh Chapel, Boston University—these are the main sources of the inspiration that has come to me through the years when preacher, congregation, and the spirit of God become involved in a moment of creative synthesis.

*Howard Thurman*

*Marsh Chapel*
*Boston*
*June 1, 1956*

# PART I

## CONCERNING ENEMIES

———— ◆◆◆ ————

## 1. LOVE YOUR ENEMIES

### MEDITATION

In ways that we can understand and in ways that transcend the farthest rim of human thought, we are mindful that God is the strength of life. As we sit together in the quietness, may we winnow enough of the essence of our own minds and spirits out of our private struggles and turmoil and needs to share our concern for the health of our President who is ill.[1] The destiny that rides on his every heartbeat is a destiny in which we all share without regard to politics or personal belief or private judgment. May we share also our concern and our anxiety and our sympathy and care that these may brood over the little community in Mississippi [2] where there is so great a burden of

[1] Reference is to the heart attack of President Eisenhower in September, 1955.
[2] The Till case in Mississippi.

1

trouble and anxiety, fear and bitterness. Grant, O God, our Father, light for our darkness, healing for our sickness, strength for our weakness, hope for our despair, forgiveness for our sins.

This is the stirring of the heart as we sit together in the quietness, each feeling the touch of each shoulder seeking the way of life, our Father.

## A DREAM OF PRAYER

I stood on the footstool of God's throne, I, a saved soul, and I saw the prayers that rose up to heaven go up before him.

And they floated up ever in new shapes and forms. And one prayed for the life of her son, and the sufferer prayed for rest, and the wronged for redress, and the poor for food, and the rich for happiness, and the lonely for love, and the loved for faith. And amid them all I saw a prayer go up that was only this: "Give me power to forgive," and it passed like a cloud of fire.

And years passed and I stood on the footstool of God's throne again and saw the prayers go up, and all were changed: he who prayed for love prayed now for power, he who prayed for ease prayed now for strength, she who had prayed for her son prayed now for his child; but I noted one prayer that went up unchanged: "Give me power to forgive."

Again years passed and I stood on the footstool of God's throne once more, and saw the prayers go up. Then among them all I noted one I knew; it said only: "Give me power to forgive."

And years passed and I stood there again. And the prayers ascended, and were all changed. And I heard a prayer, faint and low, which said: "Teach me to forgive." And I said, "Surely this may be granted now," for the voice grew weak.

# CONCERNING ENEMIES

*And God said: "It is answered; even now I have sent Death with the message."*

—OLIVE SCHREINER

———◆———

Do not I hate them, O Lord, that
hate thee? . . .
I hate them with perfect hatred.
Psalm 139:21–22

The first part of my text comes from the unfamiliar parts of the familiar 139th Psalm. The hate section is rarely read in public service. The full text is:

Do not I hate them, O Lord, that hate thee?
and am not I grieved with those that rise up against thee?
I hate them with perfect hatred:
I count them mine enemies.

Our thinking together will deal with just the first part of it. What kind of hatred is perfect hatred? Whole hatred. Complete hatred. Hatred, hatred! It is important to say at once that *hate is against life.* It is against goodness. It is against rightness. It is against God. It destroys the mind. It disintegrates the spirit. It not only isolates the individual from his fellows, but also in some strange and mysterious way it ruptures the individual's communion with God. Hatred is evil.

It is a curious thing that ideas and concepts, even emotions, seem to have a private life of their own, a private economy. They have their own etiquette, their own structure. They seem sometimes to be organisms. An idea which is planted in the mind begins to develop an autonomy which draws upon all of the energies of the nervous system to feed it, sustain it, and to make it come to fruition, independent of the house in which it lives. That is why we must always be careful of the ideas which we get into the mind. They grow and develop without reference to the ends which we are seeking.

Hatred is such an idea, such a mood, such an emotion. It has its own morality, its own private life, its own source of nurture, its own evolution. Sometimes it begins in a quiet shimmer of resentment, just a quiver that moves through the spirit as one faces something that does violence to his inner sensibility. But this resentment grows. It begins to establish its root system and its trunk system until it takes the form of hostility. It is more robust now. For hostility does not exist in a vacuum, hostility cannot be just hostility in general. It has to be focused on something. Sometimes the source of the resentment is actually the object of one's love and affection; or it may be the curious result of one's moral conviction. Then one cannot entertain any notion of hostility toward such an individual without feeling guilty; and guilt is one of the vitamins upon which hostility feeds and grows strong. If this hostility cannot express itself toward anybody else, then it is like a boomerang and turns upon its possessor.

It is very interesting to see how this acts. A man who cannot express his hostility toward the man for whom he works, because he might lose his job, may be motivated to express his hostility toward his automobile when it won't start. Or he may take out his feeling upon his son who makes a lot of noise, or upon his daughter, or upon his wife. They are close, they are available, they are vulnerable. When these escape, the individual takes it out on himself. Hostility may take the form of migraine headaches, or a lame foot, or a weak eye.

The logic of hostility as it fulfills itself moves on. It becomes hatred; and hatred is an organism. It cannot be exorcised by generous quotations, by wooing the love of another. It has to be

4

understood first. For hatred, again and again in individual life and in the collective life of man, becomes one of the very terrifying sources for reinforcing and for validating the personality. It serves often to support the sagging self-respect that an individual has when he finds himself in an environment that is overwhelming, and against which he has no protection. He retreats within himself; burrows out a hole in which to live, and takes cover; his hatred, bitter and terrible, gives him endurance. It puts cunning in his mind. It explores hidden resources of his personality. It affirms his significance, the clues to which had been obliterated by the evil with which he was trying to cope.

In this evolutionary process, hatred becomes one of the sources of our pride when all other sources have disappeared. It becomes a source of self-respect when no amount of projection can locate any other spot upon which self-respect may land and be nurtured and sustained. This is an important act in the drama of human life. What can we do about it?

We must see clearly that, even though all these things may be said about hatred, there is a most important similarity between hate and love. Both are positive; but *hatred is positive and destructive*, while *love is positive and creative*. To balance the positive similarity, there is that crucial difference. Now, after saying this, it is important to say something else. One has to deal with hatred. Religion insists that it is necessary for the healthy individual to come to grips with the personal factors and forces that surround him. If he seeks to be true to his God, to his commitment, and to the spirit of rebirth and regeneration that has taken place within him, he must never renounce the fateful moment in which he decided, with all of his passionate endeavor: "From this day forward, I will live for God, God helping me!"

Two suggestions. First, in dealing with hatred, I must seek to discover the kind of gentle wisdom that enables me to see my hatred in a *causal perspective*. This means I must understand that individuals are the creatures of training, background, culture, of personal frustrations and collective frustrations. They are the victims of all the forces that play upon their lives, shaping and modeling and fashioning them. I must understand this! The moment I am able to locate my hatred within a causal perspective, a kind of gentle religious wisdom begins to take possession of me. The hated one is ever a victim of the predicament of his life! This does not excuse him, but it helps me understand him.

Second, I recognize that I am not without guilt. The vision of God enables me to see that the roots of the hatred are in me also. When I look into the eyes of a violent man, I see myself. The moment I do this, a miracle takes place. The first fruit of hatred is isolation, and now my isolation is broken. Once more both my enemy and I stand in immediate candidacy to become members of the family.

Hatred is destructive but positive. If hatred finally destroys the individual, it is because an evil that operated on the outside shifts its basis of operation from outside to inside. When that happens, the soul of man is poisoned. May God have mercy on his predicament.

———◆———

*Accept, O God, the struggle of the mind and the feeble conscientious effort of the spirit to reveal truth and light as the offering which we bring and place with great gentleness upon Thy altar. Dismiss us with Thy Spirit, and desert us not in the lonely way that we may take as we seek to find Thy truth in the midst of error.*

6

# 2. CONFRONTING THE ENEMY—I

*Golden indeed is it to welcome the return of the period of quiet in the midst of all by which we are surrounded; to have moments of solitariness in the midst of community, when we may dare to reveal ourselves to God. What great relief comes from being under no necessity to pretend anything, to have no awareness of the service that the alibi can give; but in the quietness to finger one by one the pieces that go to make up one's life, to expose them in utter honesty and integrity before the scrutiny and the love of God. The weaknesses, the strength, the heartaches, the heart balms, the anxieties and the tranquillities, the good and the evil, the desires and ambitions and dreams and hopes, we finger them, we turn them over, one by one, before God.*

7

This we do, our Father, seeking only the gift of Thy understanding, the trust of Thy love, and the strength of Thy judgment.

Let the words of our mouths and the meditations of our hearts be acceptable in Thy sight, O Lord, our rock and our redeemer.

### READING

O Thou in whose hand our breath is, show patience and judge me not according to my words of angry reproach and bitterness, wild words, flying out half meant, often, from a thing in pain! For even as I chide Thee and renounce Thee, I know that Thou must be judged by all space and all time and not by any one man's life, least of all by any hot and displeased part of it. Also I know that there is, that there can be, no other way for a man than that he answer to truth, rightly and honorably, before his own soul and Thee, whatever comes. This stands, must ever stand, though seasons change, and flesh protest, and circumstance cry havoc, and all else but this be gone. Hold me to my course, O unknown Captain, despite wintry weather! Nay, grant me courage and a true heart that I myself may hold myself to my course! Ride with me on the waves, and speak brave words of heartening, and, if I am to be engulfed, may it be with my way still set by the fixed north star!

—OSWALD W. S. McCALL

We turn our minds to the matter of confronting an enemy. When I say that a man is my enemy, I mean at once that he is ethically out of bounds—out of bounds to any moral demands that he can make upon me, or to any demands that I might otherwise make upon him. It is instructive to examine the teaching of Jesus on the treatment of such a person.

The first enemy with whom Jesus deals is common to all human relationships. Perhaps the word "enemy" is too strong, but at any rate, he was thinking of primary human relationships. The personal enemy! Who is he? An individual bound to us in intimate ways, but, because of what he has done or said, one who has ruptured this relationship. He is a friend who has acted in a manner that is purposefully unfriendly and who, by that action, has introduced into our relationship something that is divisive and destructive. We all have had such experiences, both as the offender and as the injured person. Jesus taught that if I go before God to present my gift to Him and there, in the moment of silence before Him, I remember that all is not well between me and somebody else, I must leave my gift without presenting it. The gift must wait. I must first find the individual from whom there is estrangement. I must work out the details of reconciliation. I must restore the lost harmony. Only after this has happened may I return to offer my gift. This is Jesus' teaching! It is often difficult to follow. I do not have enough wisdom to know the reasons why it is so difficult. Perhaps I hesitate to seek reconciliation because, in the seeking, I myself become too vulnerable. Perhaps I fear that as I pass over to the offender the withering effect of my judgment against him, I may see shining clearly in the light of my self-righteousness the very thing in me that triggered the deed in him. I hesitate to run that risk. But the instruction is unequivocal. When I have a personal enemy with whom my sense of community has been ruptured, I must put aside my blindness, my conceit, my arrogance. I must find the person, talk it through, feel it through, think it through, and arrive at a climate of understanding that absorbs the rupture and restores the primary intimate character of our relationship. When I have done that, then I can go before my God in one piece.

Is there anybody with whom you are out of harmony today? As we sit here this morning, offering our prayers to God, do you see the face of someone who comes between you and God? It may be that you feel you have the right to be out of harmony because you know you have never done to anybody what was done to you. Yet you must find a way to love your enemy if you want to be whole; not if you want to redeem your enemy, but because you want to be whole. A part of you is caught in the deed which he has done and you must get you out of it to restore wholeness to yourself.

There is a second kind of enemy. He is a man who is a part of our group life. For any one of a wide variety of reasons, he opens the door to the common enemy. Such a person in the experience and life of Jesus was the tax collector. Here was a man who was a member of the Jewish community and who knew the local psychology; but in accepting the position and the pay of an oppressive government, he rented his knowledge to that government. He took his knowledge as one would a can opener and pressed it into the hands of the Romans. He exploited his own community and opened the door to the enemy.

Among the new words that came into our vocabulary as a result of the second World War is the word "quisling." Why did the man whose name we use with contempt do the thing he did? The causal question is always relevant. Why? Was it because he was ashamed of his community? Did he want to escape from all the penalties and judgments that society had passed upon him as a member of that community? Was that the reason? Or was it because he felt that the struggle for place, for position, for status, within the community was so tremendous that he could not possibly achieve a victory? One thing that he could do was to step out from among his fellows and align himself with those whose existence was a threat to the total community. What he could not experience in terms of self-respect, self-regard, and self-esteem as a member of the community, he could experience through being placed in a preferred position by those who were able to pass out status and recognition. Perhaps he needed money desperately; this is a thing that can be understood, though not condoned. He may have said, "I do not mean to be a bad man, I need the money." He had no interest in selling the community short, he just wanted to take care of his family. He acted according to what at the moment seemed to him the normal fulfillment of his economic responsibilities. But the relentless logic of the actions which seemed to guarantee his own economic security meant the betrayal of the community.

Two things must be done for the tax collector who comes into my life. First, I must lose my fear of him. I must reduce the psychological distance between me and him. This Jesus did by associating with him. This was taking a long step because it exposed Jesus to the bitter judgment of guilt by association. In the second thing that Jesus did we see the full-orbed genius of the Son of Man. The tax collector must be made aware of the fact that he, the tax collector, was a son of Abraham. How tremendous was this insight of Jesus. The first thing that the man had to get rid of in order to be a tax collector was an awareness that he was a son of Abraham, that he was a member of the community in good standing, with roots as deep as life. He had to wipe that out of his consciousness before he could rent himself to the government. Jesus suggests that he must be reminded of his rightful place in the community and that he must be made to face the thing that has caused him to forget what he is. Once that has been done, then for the first time he is in a position to deal with his moral problem. It can't be done merely by judging him. When I deal with a man in such a situation, I

11

must re-establish in him the sense of community that he had lost. I can't do that if I don't love him!

"Love your enemy that you may become children of your Father who is in heaven, who causes the rain to fall on the good man and the bad man, and his sun to shine on the just and the unjust."

To love my enemy is to seek for the perfection which is not of God but in God.

---❖---

*We are grateful, our Father, for the light which Thou dost cast upon our pathway, illuminating the deepest darkness in which our souls go astray. Dismiss us from this place, but leave us not, as we seek this day, and tomorrow, and tomorrow, and tomorrow, to find the way, the truth, and the life.*

# 3. CONFRONTING THE ENEMY—II

## MEDITATION

There is a strange wonder in the beauty of a healthy human relationship. Such a relationship can never be fitted into a pattern of logic or into one of orderly order. This is not to ignore the causal element or to pass by the part that the rational and deliberate aspects of mind play in bringing into being the delight that one human being finds or discovers in another. Of course there is planning, there is understanding, there is a studied element in the behavior. It is this element that has been overlooked too often in the attempt to achieve healthy human relationships. The tendency to by-pass the other person's facts in a head-on drive to relate, is the great besetting sin of those who work for healthy human relations out of detached incentives or out of compulsions inspired by commitments in which the other person is not involved. Whatever may be the quality of a man's devotion to goals of health and understanding among his fellows—if within the sweeping intensity of that devotion the other person's facts are not included, the result is fatal and sometimes terrifying. For it means that the other persons are used as means to ends in which they do not consciously share and in which they are not privileged to participate.

The wonder in the beauty of a healthy human relationship is due in large part to a quality inherent in human personality. For lack of a better term, let it be called the Quality of Intimacy. For some it is possessed in grand and exciting abundance. All who come within their ken are warmed and glowed by this Presence. For some it means much trial and much error—they have a clumsiness that makes of the simplest relationship a hardship. Such persons are often the last to understand why it is that there seems to be no resemblance between what they feel in their hearts about their fellows and what they are able to achieve. The Quality of Intimacy is constantly ambushed by a failure to understand the other person's facts. For others the Quality of Intimacy is exploited and turned into a weapon of violence making a wilderness of despair out of a beautiful meadow.

The dream of a friendly world, of friendly men, beneath a friendly sky—in fine, the dream of healthy human relationships cannot be left to chance. There must ever be an abundance of study, understanding, experimentation. All of these things, however, are of no avail if the magic of the Quality of Intimacy is not released to illumine, to hallow, to make whole. The Quality of Intimacy is the shaft of light coming from Him who lighteth every man who cometh into the world.

# IN MEMORIAM, EMMETT TILL

In Mississippi the murder of fourteen-year-old Emmett Till still goes unpunished. It will be punished, nevertheless, for there is a higher law than Mississippi's.

Emmett Till was a child. One of the country's traditions is the religion of Jesus, who said: "But whosoever shall offend one of these little ones which believe in me, it were better for him that a millstone were hanged about his neck, and that he were drowned in the depth of the sea."

Men can be forgiven for prejudice, as a sign of ignorance or imperfect understanding of their religion; no righteous man can condone a brutal murder. Those in Sumner, and elsewhere who do condone it, are in far worse danger than Emmett Till ever was. He had only his life to lose, and many others have done that, including his soldier-father, who was killed in France fighting for the American proposition that all men are equal. Those who condone a deed so foul as this are in danger of losing their own souls.

The soul of Emmett Till himself was known but to few but it was a thing of value. It was fashioned on July 25, 1941, by the Lord God Almighty who placed on it this distinctive seal:

This is My son, akin to all others, but unlike any one of them. Like each of My children he is unique, irreplaceable, immortal. I hereby send him among other men, who are his brothers.

He went, and was slain. In the dark night of this deed his childish cries for mercy fell on deaf ears. But they were heard, nonetheless, and God made an entry, that night, "It must needs be that offenses come, but woe to that man by whom the offense cometh."

*Sleep well, Emmett Till; you will be remembered as long as men have tongues to cry against evil. It is true now as it was when Christ said it almost 2000 years ago: "For there is nothing covered that shall not be revealed; neither hid that shall not be known. . . . Whatsoever you have spoken in darkness shall be heard in the light. . . . Be not afraid of them that kill the body. . . . Fear him, which after he hath killed hath power to cast into hell. . . . Are not five sparrows sold for two farthings, and not one of them is forgotten before God? . . .*

*"Fear not, therefore, ye are of more value than many sparrows."*

—Life magazine

———◆———

We turn now to the third kind of enemy, the political and social enemy. In the experience of Jesus, this was Rome.

Either Jesus as he lived in Palestine resented the domination and the control of the Roman government or he consciously did not resent it. It would be altogether unreasonable to assume that he could be indifferent to it. What must he do about Rome? This question had to be settled before he could get to other questions, such as: What shall I do with my life? What must be the behavior toward an enemy of one who feels himself to be in some strikingly peculiar sense the Son of God? Similarly, what must I do about my enemy?

We remind ourselves that by definition the enemy is one who is ethically out of bounds for us. Let us bring this statement into focus and think about it. Why is it that when a nation goes to war with us, one of the first things that happens is a redefinition of the status, character, private life, public life, history, culture, of the people that we are fighting? We redefine them out of the human race. The German people become the Huns.

The Japanese become those hideous creatures with buck teeth and horrible eyes surrounded by huge glasses. By redefinition we read them out of the human family. Once that is done, it is open season. We can do anything to them without violating the sensitive, ethical awareness that goes with our own sense of self-respect.

We see this same tendency simply expressed in a personal dimension. For instance, you may be one of those who cannot say to other people exactly what you think of them until you lose your temper. You know how that is. When you lose your temper, you seem to gain an immunity from inner disintegration, and you can say what you wouldn't feel free enough to say, if you had not lost your temper first. So you lose your temper. You leave your self-respect intact behind the temper; then you come around in front to say all the things you want to say. Then you go back and again pick up your self-respect. Now exactly this same thing is done when we redefine the public enemy. If I can ever say that the enemy is not worthy of being a member of the human race, if I can say that he has behaved in a manner that shows that he is not human, I feel relieved of any responsibility to deal with him within my context of ethical awareness.

Jesus, however, approaches life from the point of view of God. The serious problem for him had to be: Is the Roman a child of God? Is my enemy God's child? If he is, I must work upon myself until I am willing to bring him back into the family. Does God love him? It doesn't help me any to say, I am not God. That would be convenient but irrelevant. If God loves him, that binds me. Can it be that God does not know how terrible he is? No, God knows him as well as he knows himself and much better than I know him. It must be true, then, that there is something in every man that remains intact, inviolate, regardless of what he does. I wonder! Is this true? Is there an integrity of the person, so intrinsic in its value and significance that no deed, however evil, can ultimately undermine this given thing. If a man is of infinite worth in the sight of God, whether he is saint or sinner, whether he is a good man or a bad man, evil or not, if that is true, then I am never relieved of my responsibility for trying to make contact with this worthy thing in him. I must love him because God causes the sun to shine upon him as well as upon me.

It must also be observed that every person does belong to the human family, to the family of God. No deed that he does, therefore, however awful it may be is completely indicative of all that there is to him and in him. Now I am perfectly willing to apply that judgment to myself; to say that the thing I did to you was terrible but that I wasn't altogether present and accounted for in the deed; that some margin of me was unexpressed and that my real self was not in all this. Jesus recognizes that every man, even the Roman, is caught in the limitation of his own kind of predicament. Let us illustrate this point.

A Roman captain came to Jesus one day and said to him, "Sir, will you help me? I have a servant who is very close to my heart, and that servant has the palsy and he is in great distress of body and mind. I have tried all kinds of help and nothing has reached him and touched his need. Will you please heal him?"

Now what do you think must have gone on in the mind of this Roman to ready him so that he could run the risk as a Roman of asking this Jewish teacher for help? Think of the number of doubts he must have had: "What will my soldiers say; what will the commanding officer say; what will my friends say if they know that I put myself at the mercy of this Jewish teacher?" Jesus said, "I will go to your house." And very quickly the captain said, "Oh, no, that isn't necessary." He didn't say "That isn't necessary" because he didn't want the Jewish teacher in his house. Think of it! He was free enough in his approach to Jesus to know that he would not be misunderstood when he said, "No, it really isn't necessary for you to go to my house." He was confident that Jesus did not think, "Oh, yes, you want me to help you but you don't want me to be seen with you. You want me to help you by remote control, at a great distance so that there will be no embarrassment." He was free enough to say to Jesus, "It isn't necessary for you to go to my house because you are in such vital contact with the limitless resources of God that all you need to do is to pour out your compassion and it can reach to the ends of the earth and heal what it touches."

Jesus said about him, "I have not found such faith as this in all my teaching."

Now what had actually happened? The Roman soldier represented the enemy in the social experience and the historical experience of Jesus; he had to get out from under his "Roman predicament." Jesus, the Jewish teacher, had to get out from under his "Jewish predicament." The two human spirits, now relieved of the burden of their predicaments, were free at last to deal with each other as children of God.

A man cannot love his enemy until he is able to restore his enemy to good standing in the human family. He may pray for him, may serve him, he may flagellate himself in atonement because he cannot like the man; he may respond with retaliation and resentment and hostility. But he can't love him until emotionally he is able to get him outside a context that binds him and defines him. He must recognize him as a child of God, as a member of the family of God. That is why loving one's enemy demands an insight that is more religious than ethical and moral.

One important aspect of the subject is still untouched. What, as a human being, can I do about all the pain that I have when armies run over my land, destroy my family, desecrate what is precious to me? What shall I do with that? How can I handle it? I don't know the whole answer. I must understand that life provides its own restraint; that the relentless logic of the moral order, grounded in the structure of existence, will see to it that every man, every man must sometime sit down and look into the eyes of his evil deed. No man escapes. Life is its own restraint and when I attempt to become the avenger, I am merely crying out my agony in the nighttime. No man can truly take vengeance upon another man. Only God in His intimate involvement in the very heart and life of all of His children can bring to pass the relentless logic of the moral law. It is not whistling in the dark when Jesus says, "Love your enemies and pray for those who persecute you, so that you may be sons of your Father who is in heaven [with whom vengeance rests]." "Vengeance is mine," says the Book. God is not only the God of Religion, but He is also the God of Life. When I love my enemy, I come closest to the perfection which is God. When I do this, I resist the temptation to act as a member of the human race with special privileges. Love your enemy. Love your enemy. Love your enemy, and so fulfill the Will of God, in you.

———◆———

With a certain sense of shame and limitation, but with enthusiasm of spirit, we make to Thee, O God, the offering of our minds and spirits. Be with us as we move each one of us into the pattern of the daily responsibility of life, and may nothing separate us from Thy love today, and tomorrow, and tomorrow, and tomorrow, O God, the Father of our spirits.

# 4. THE GREATEST OF THESE

"While there is a lower class,
    I am in it;
While there is a criminal element,
    I am of it;
While there is a man in jail,
    I am not free."
Thus spoke one whose very life and deeds
These words fulfilled.
Contacts with one another abound in a world grown small,
Because the mind of man has worked unceasingly to
Banish barriers set by nature, here and there;
Everywhere.
But where there is no will to love, to make an act

**21**

Of grace toward fellow men,
Contacts may degrade, outrage—nip
The tender shoots of simple trust.
Love abides when all else sickens and dies
From sheer revulsion and disgust.
The fruit it bears sustains the nerve and makes the life
A harbor of repose for the weak and tottering;
A heavy judgment for the cruel and hating;
A "precious bane" for those who seek to know
The way of God among the sons of men.
With it, the deeds of men are measured
By man's great destiny.
It meets men where they are—sometimes cruel,
Sometimes lustful, sometimes greedy;
Often callous, mean, of low design,—
And treats them there, as if they were full grown
And crowned with all that God would have them be.
For love's sake and love's alone, men do with joyous hope
And tender joy what no command of Heaven,
Hell or Life could force of them
If love were not.
To be God's child, to love with steady mind
And fervent heart . . . this,
This is the Law of Love.

READING

# WHEN THE STRAIN IS HEAVIEST

At times when the strain is heaviest upon us,
And our tired nerves cry out in many-tongued pain
Because the flow of love is choked far below the deep recesses
    of the heart,

22

We seek with cravings firm and hard
The strength to break the dam
That we may live again in love's warm stream.
We want more love; and more and more
Until, at last, we are restored and made anew!
Or, so it seems.

When we are closer drawn to God's great Light
And in its radiance stand revealed,
The meaning of our need informs our minds.
"More love," we cried; as if love could be weighed, measured,
    bundled, tied.
As if with perfect wisdom we could say—to one, a little love;
    to another, an added portion;
And on and on until all debts were paid
With no one left behind.

But now we see the tragic blunder of our cry.
Not for more love our hungry cravings seek!
But more power to love.
To put behind the tender feeling, the understanding heart,
The boundless reaches of the Father's Care
Makes love eternal, always kindled, always new.
This becomes the eager meaning of the aching heart
The bitter cry—the anguish call!

◆

> And now abideth faith, hope,
> love, these three; but the
> greatest of these is love.
>
> I Corinthians 13:13

There are some people who by temperament, by constitution, by glandular function seem to be naturally outgoing. A quality of spontaneity envelopes their personality and it reaches out and enfolds the other person. But for the most part, love is a discipline. A discipline! The discipline is rooted, as far as our personalities are concerned, in desire. There must be actively at work in the personality the desire to love, for this desire is the dynamic, the energy, the ceaseless rhythmic pulse that sustains the enterprise of the conscious mind. Again and again we discover, as we look at X or Y or Z, that the truth is we don't want to love him. We know that we ought to want to love him, but we don't want to. So we use a lot of phrases, such as: "I will love him for Christ's sake, but I don't like him."

This first basic step is very radical. I must want to love; I must desire *to desire* to love. Here I feel that the primary relationship of the individual with God is of the greatest importance and significance in the whole etiquette and morality and experience of love. I must offer to God my continuum of desires, expose them to the loving power of His spirit until at last there emerges in the very ground of the feeling tones of my life the focusing, the rallying, the pointing of my desires in this regard. If I am to think and feel and experience love, I must search deep within me and relate myself to my God in whose Presence I expose all of me. When this is done, there does emerge in the body of my desires this special desire to love.

Now I am ready to get into my hands a tool that will enable me to implement my desires. Here the will comes in, the mind, the formal intensive processes of mind! I offer to my redirection, or my focused desires, the hard core of my decision. I now am able to make up my mind. And I now deliver to the dynamics of my personality the energy of will. There begins to emerge in me the will to love and the will to love becomes an

24

organizing principle. It becomes a structuring principle, so that my desire *to desire* can be extended, implemented, developed. Where there is no will to love, the personality is unmanageable in this regard. The will to love has to be nourished, has to be fed, has to be related to an energy, or else it cannot be activated in the midst of all the vicissitudes of my living and my experiencing.

Once I have done this, there is another quality that I must put into the hands of my focused feeling tones, my focused desires, and that is another aspect of mind. For lack of a better term, I call it imagination. I must contrive some way by which I can dally with the other person. To use a colloquial term, I must "fool around" with the other person's personality. When my imagination is brought into play, as one of the additional tools for the implementation of my desiring, certain things begin to happen. I become able to project myself, first in little ways, into the other person's life, into the other person's situation. I am able to do that even as I remain myself.

A simple and dramatic illustration of this comes to my mind. I was visiting a friend of mine whose little boy had just learned to ride his kiddy cart. He rode it into the living room, and stopped at my feet and said, "Mr. Thurman, will you help me change my tire? I just had a blowout." I put my newspaper down. I helped him jack up the car. We took the old tire off and put the new one on. We put the jack back where it belonged. Then he sat in his car and tried to start the motor, but it didn't start. He pulled out the choke, then stepped on the starter; again nothing happened. He got out, lifted up one side of the hood and tinkered around. "Everything is all right here." He went around to the other side. "Everything is all right on this side." He got back into the car and stepped on the starter, but nothing happened. Then he began talking to his car, using language he had heard his father use under such circumstances. Still, nothing happened. Finally he said, "Maybe I don't have any gasoline." He got out, came over to me and said, "Do you have a pencil, Mr. Thurman?" I said, "Yes," and gave him a pencil. He took the top off the tank, put the pencil down into the tank, held it up and said, "Ah! The tank is empty." He returned the pencil. He went to the kitchen, got a glass of water from his mother, came back, sat down again in his kiddy cart, drank the water, started his motor and drove out of the living room into the kitchen.

There must be this sense of self-projection that enables me to move into the context in which the other person is living and look out on the common situation through the other person's eyes, even as I remain myself. When I do that, I make very important discoveries about this other person, discoveries which now inform my will and make it the major tool for the implementation of my desires. The use of imagination in this way gives me a sense of the right thing to say to precipitate the free flow of the good, healthy feeling that binds me to the other person and the other to me. I have begun to understand him, to know why he does the things he does.

Sometimes, simple mechanical devices can be resorted to as aids to understanding. A young couple in my church in San Francisco worked out a very simple device. Whenever the husband came home from work in the late afternoon, and was upset or irritable, he would leave his handkerchief dangling out of his jacket pocket. When his wife saw this, she knew that this was not a good day to do anything that was not just within the zones of harmonious agreement. On the other hand, if she had on a certain apron that he had given her, he knew that this was not her day. Simple! We must study ways and means to release our desires that they may go home to their goals. It cannot be left to chance, it cannot be left to accident, it cannot be left to some kind of overbrooding sentimentality. It requires a discipline. The human spirit and personality must work at it . . . work at it . . . work at it. The will to love must not be dammed up and blocked by things that could be removed if we took the time to think.

There is another service of imagination as a tool. It is illustrated in the Biblical record of a certain woman who was taken in adultery. The men who brought her to Jesus said, "Master, we caught this woman in the act of adultery. The law says she should be stoned to death. What do you say inasmuch as you declare that you came to fulfill the law, not to destroy it? What do you say? Do you ignore the law? What do you say?" And Jesus said, "Let the man among you who is without spot or blemish cast the first stone. After that, anybody may throw." And he wrote on the ground. After what seemed an eternity, I imagine, he lifted his face and looked at the woman. He had not looked at her before. He was a gentleman. He did not want his eyes to be mingled with the eyes of those who sat in judgment upon her. "Woman, where are they? Does no man condemn thee?"

"No, no, no . . ."

"Neither do I. Go, go into peace. And don't do it any more."

He met her where she was, admittedly an adulteress. He didn't slough that over. He met her where she was, but he treated her there, where she was, as if she were where she should have been. By so doing, he lifted her into the fulfillment of her personality.

I can love only when I meet you where you are, as you are, and treat you there as if you were where you ought to be. I see you where you are, striving and struggling, and in the light of the highest possibility of your personality, I deal with you there.

My own religious faith is insistent that this can be done only out of a life of devotion. I must cultivate the inner spiritual resources of my life to such a point that I can bring you to my sanctuary, before His Presence, until, at last, I do not know you from myself. The discipline of the heart and the mind and the desire may become a lung through which God breathes. Therefore, if I say I love God and don't love you—I lie. If I say I love you and don't love God—I lie.

Now abideth faith, hope, and love. The greatest of these is love.

———◆———

*Teach me, O God, our Father, that I may desire to desire to love; that my will may become the active servant in the hands of my desire; that my imagination may be the vehicle through which my will now disciplines my life and orders my environment to the end that I may be Thy child in the midst of Thy children.*

*Let the words of our mouths and the meditations of our hearts be acceptable in Thy sight, O God—God, our Rock and our Redeemer.*

# PART II

## CONCERNING PRAYER

───────◆───────

# 1. TEACH US TO PRAY

### MEDITATION

There is something strangely comforting and reassuring about the private pretensions under which we live. It is a matter of no little significance to know that for each of us there is a world apart in which the intimacy of thoughts and feelings may be safe from attack and violation. Much of what we mean by communication is limited to the deliberate choosing of thoughts, ideas, sentiments, feelings, which we direct toward others—yielding only the meaning that we intend, which may not be the meaning that is either true or honest. In time we develop a dependence upon the impact which we make on others as the major source upon which we draw for an understanding of ourselves.

I am impressed by the accounts which have come to us concerning the life of the American Indian at a time far removed from the present. To him, so the accounts reveal, the Great Spirit brooded over all of life in general and particular. If he went hunting, prior to the journey, he invoked the Great Spirit. When crops were planted, when there were death and birth—in fine, all the common and special experiences of life were seen as being under the scrutiny and sponsorship of the Great Spirit. This meant that there was ever available the opportunity and the necessity for being genuine—the wall between the inner and the outer was very thin and transparent. The integrity of the act sprung out of the integrity of the person. With reference to so much of the common life, there was no need to pretend. One dare not pretend to the Great Spirit.

A crushing part of the sophistication of modern life is the phenomenal rise in the feeling for a protective covering that will make the integrity of the act an awkward procedure. Why is it that we are embarrassed by simple honesty and directness in our communication with one another? And yet the hunger deepens and becomes more and more insistent for ridding ourselves of the tremendous burden of pretensions. We long for relationships in which it is no longer needful for us to pretend anything. The clue to the answer is in the awakening within us of the sense of living our lives consciously in God's presence. The habit of exposing the life, the motives, the dreams, the desires, the sins, all, to God makes for the Integrity of the Person out of which there will flow more and more the Integrity of the Act.

> Search me, O God, and know my Heart,
> Try me and know my Thoughts.

# THE ADVENTURE OF PRAYER

*Prayer is being with God.*

*You can't choose at all about it, except just in choosing to be with Him.*

*Perhaps He will take you up on the mountain with Him.*

*Perhaps He will take you into the night with Him, or into the mist where you will not be able to see Him.*

*Perhaps you will be with Him in pain, or in exaltation, or in happiness, or in tiredness.*

*He just says: "Come to Me," and you say: "I will," or "I will not."*

You make no stipulations, that is not your part; you know that He wants you, and you know what kind of wanting that is.

You know that if you say you will not come He does not leave off wanting you, so you imagine what that means.

You know that if you come to Him He will ask you to help Him about the Kingdom, that He will in the end give you that work for it that no one else can do.

You know that He will bring you into the Fellowship of His friends, and that you will be allowed to bring Him into the Fellowship of your friends.

But, of course, you will also go with Him before His enemies; and the things that they say about Him will be said about you.

And you will also go among the people who don't care, whom He is trying to arouse to a sense of His Love.

Quite often He and you will be left desolate with the doors locked before you and the people on the other side scornful and amused.

You will find that He will ask you to do things which you can only do if you forget about yourself and the sort of person you thought you were, or He may ask you to face death or complete shame as He does Himself.

And all the time you will fail Him so often that by and by you will have no self-confidence left, only a growing confidence in Him instead, because He does not fail you.

And prayer must be fearfully difficult because it isn't easy to be with God, although it is simple.

It means that some things must go, like pride, unkindness, and self-indulgence, and self-importance.

But all the same it is a choice which the best part of you wants, so that the most glorious souls in all the ages do choose the Adventure of Prayer.

—MARGARET CROPPER

——◆——

Lord, teach us to pray. . . .
Luke 11:1

It is of very great significance to me that the only specific request the disciples of Jesus made of him for themselves was the request concerning prayer. "Lord, teach us to pray." This is important because it suggests that it was in the area of his religious experience, in the area of his experience with God, that Jesus was most utterly compelling. So compelling was he that with unerring insight his disciples put their hands on this key to the meaning of his life, the accent, the flavor of his power and contagion.

The basic proposition underlying our need for prayer is this: We wish never to be left, literally, to our own resources. Again and again, we discover that our own resources are not equal to the demands of our living. We are made to realize this in many ways. We know that we are not self-contained. We know how utterly dependent we are upon so many things around us. Our dependence upon those we know, and upon many whom we do not know, is evident. How contingent our present life is upon life that has gone before! In the simplest aspects of our living, we see this demonstrated. Consider the words we use—yes, even our alphabet. How long it must have taken our forebears, somewhere, in some way, to fashion simple things like the alphabets out of which words are made. And the words we use? What a story they have to tell about the involvement of hundreds of thousands of minds and spirits, in successes and failures, in heartaches and trepidations, before at last, language, the miracle of communication, became possible. Thus, it is obvious that, in literal truth, we cannot be left entirely to our own resources. We do not often, however, apply our sense of dependence to our personal relationships to God. What is the most dramatic utterance that we make when pressure bears down upon us? We cry out Something to Somebody. Sometimes we do it in conventional ways, and sometimes in ways that are not quite conventional. But in dire necessity we always recognize the poverty of our little lives. We feel that we can't go on alone if left to our little resources, however powerful we may seem to be at other times.

Now prayer is one of the most searching, and I think one of the most comprehensive, methods for tapping resources that are beyond ourselves. We tap such resources in behalf of our own needs and to banish the shadows that cross our paths. We tap such resources in behalf of the needs of others. Again and again men may find themselves unable to ask for help in their own behalf, but, at the same time, they do not hesitate to ask it in behalf of the objects of their affection, or the objects of their concern. Often a man who will not pray for himself, who will not seek to relate himself to some source that can confirm and renew and revitalize his own life, will be most humble and most abject in his effort to pray for his loved one, if his loved one is threatened.

It is possible to draw upon resources beyond ourselves. You will recall the man to whom Jesus said, "This can be done, if you have faith." And the man replied, "I have faith, help thou my lack of faith." It is as part of the awareness of faith itself that the sense of the lack of faith arises. The resource that is within us is the clue to the resource that is beyond ourselves, and this we tap in the experience of prayer. Some years ago, Irwin Edman wrote a book called *Richard Kane Looks at Life*. It is a series of letters between a philosophy professor and a rather precocious student. The student was conscious of some inner insecurity and tried in various ways to find the meaning of life. At length he wrote to the professor saying that in spite of his efforts to solve his problems, the quest was still going on; he had not been able to find what he sought. Perhaps, he said, it was God he was seeking, after all. The professor in his reply suggested that the hunger itself was God. The thing within me is also that which is without. I tap the resource that is beyond me by making conscious contact with the resource that is within me. "The beyond is within" is the way Plotinus puts it.

Now, if this presents a true picture, then some preparation is very much in order. It takes time to learn how to tap the resources that are beyond ourselves. And we are all in a hurry. Our lives are moving at a rapid rate. We cannot reach to the support we need if we do not take time to "ready" our spirits, to prepare ourselves. We must have time for quiet and some place where we can have an atmosphere of quiet outside, before what is outside begins to move inside our consciousness.

In my first church there was a certain lady who sat about four rows from the front each Sunday morning. She always went to sleep. She would manage to stay awake until after the hymn before the offering and the doxology. Then she settled down and slept until the benediction. I went to call on her husband who was ill. On my way out of the house, she walked with me to the door. As I was about to go down the steps she said to me: "I know you wonder why I sleep every Sunday during your sermon. There are two reasons. The first is that it takes you so long to say what you want to say, and I simply give up; I find it too exhausting to listen to you. And the second reason is that I am so tired." As I listened, I took in her situation and said, "Now that I have visited your home and seen the kind of turmoil in which you live six and a half or seven days a week, I feel that the greatest contribution the church can make to you is to provide a quiet place, once a week, in which you can sit down and go to sleep in peace."

It is important to recognize that we cannot prescribe the rules by which spiritual power is available to us. Who are we, with our little conceits, with our little arrogances, with our little madnesses, to lay down the conditions upon which we will accept the resources of life that sustain and confirm the integrity of our being? No, we must learn how to be quiet; and this takes discipline. We must find, each of us for himself, the kind of rhythmic pattern which will control our stubborn and unyielding and recalcitrant nervous systems, and nourish our spiritual concerns and our growth in grace.

———————

*Teach me to pray, O God, my Father, that I may find the rhythmic pattern of my own spirit, which will lead me to the source of all life, lest my soul perish.*

# 2. PRERYER AND SILENCE

### MEDITATION

*Whither shall I go from Thy Presence?*
*From Thee is there some hiding place?*

> *The deed is a thing so private*
> *So inside the perfect working of desire*
> *That its inward part seems known to me,*
> *To me alone.*

> *The ebb and flow of thoughts*
> *Within my hidden sea,*
> *The forms that stir within the channels of my mind,*
> *Keep tryst with all my intimate hopes and fears.*

The ties that hold me fast to those whose
Life with mine makes one,
The tangled twine that binds my life
With things I claim as mine
Seem cut off from all else but
My embrace.

The great stillness that walls around
The heartaches and the pain
Is sealed against aught else that would invade.

The awe-filled contrition emptied of all violence and all sin
Keeps watch with the spent loneliness
Of my deserted soul.

The joy crowding to the quivering brim the heights and
uppermost reaches of vast delight
Gives room to nothing but itself alone.

And yet,
Always I know that Another
Sees and understands—
Every vigil with me keeps watch—
The door through which He comes no man
Can shut—
He is the Door!

I cannot go from Thy Presence.
There is no hiding place from Thee.

# CONCERNING PRAYER

## LA VIE PROFONDE

Hemmed in by petty thoughts and petty things,
 Intent on toys and trifles all my years,
Pleased by life's gauds, pained by its pricks and stings,
 Swayed by ignoble hopes, ignoble fears;
Threading life's tangled maze without life's clue,
 Busy with means, yet heedless of their ends,
Lost to all sense of what is real and true,
 Blind to the goal to which all Nature tends:—
Such is my surface self: but deep beneath,
 A mighty actor on a world-wide stage,
Crowned with all knowledge, lord of life and death,
 Sure of my aim, sure of my heritage,—
I—the true self—live on, in self's despite,
That "life profound" whose darkness is God's light.
       —EDMOND G. A. HOLMES

To get at the core of God at his greatest, one must first get into the core of himself at his least, for no one can know God who has not first known himself. Go to the depths of the soul, the secret place of the most high, to the roots, to the heights; for all that God can do is focused there.

### and

In limpid souls God beholds his own image; he rests in them and they in him. . . . I like best those things in which I see most clearly the likeness of God. Nothing in all creation is so like God as stillness.

       —SOURCE UNKNOWN

Prayer and Silence. We are continuing the interpretation of prayer as the experience in which the individual draws upon resources beyond himself in behalf of himself, and on behalf of the interests by which that self is defined. The point of contact, the opening, through which these resources become manifest in human life is deep within human life. The process by which we work ourselves from the periphery, from the outside of ourselves, on the long journey to the floodgate within ourselves, is a part of what we mean by meditation. Quietness, stillness, silence, become very important. It is in the climate of quietness, stillness, silence, that we get release from the involvements which keep us defocused, scattered, entangled.

There is, of course, the immediate place that external quiet holds in this process. We must have a peaceful place where the physical, tangible environment can be at rest, so that the other dimensions of our lives can be brought into focus. Let me illustrate this.

Some years ago, one of my university students, who had been a deep-sea diver, wrote a very interesting sketch. In it he described one of his experiences on the Caribbean Sea. He was on the ocean bottom. It was very beautiful down there. The water was clear, and he was in the midst of a coral rock garden. Since he was in no particular hurry, he sat down to look around. He sat; he looked. Occasionally, a fish would swim up to take a close look at him and would pass the word along to his friends, who were also curious. After an indefinite time, he lost track of all time awareness. Then he discovered that he was sitting in the midst of a very beautiful flower garden. There were plants of many shapes, and things that looked like blossoms. It was wonderful. He could enjoy the beauty for a long while; but he realized that he couldn't stay there forever, so he stirred to go about his business. And, as soon as he moved, every plant disappeared. Apparently these were living things that were in mid-passage between the vegetable and animal world. They emerged only when he was completely still. That's what I mean. Take the idea. Apply it!

Now we are ready for the second step. The physical silence needs a place that doesn't even *look* noisy. We must now turn within to see if the noises, the confusion, the churning that are going on inside us can be quieted. Otto calls this "the numinous silence of waiting." It is the silence of preparation when the individual is readying himself for the movement of the spirit of the living God. This waiting mood may be encouraged in various ways, sometimes by reading a great paragraph, sometimes by repeating over and over again some significant affirmation of the human spirit. Little by little we begin to settle down, to focus within. The Quakers have developed this ability to a very marked degree—this waiting. Many of you have been to Friends' meetings, or perhaps have had a similar experience elsewhere. At first, even though no one is moving, and there is no noise anywhere, the inner ear seems to hear confusion. You *hear* it. Then more and more . . . more and more . . . more and more . . . things begin to settle, to shake down. At what point, you don't know, but you do become involved in the stillness, in the quietness. Something begins breathing through the stillness, communicating to your mind and to your spirit, meeting your individual need at the level of your need. Let me illustrate this.

Once I traveled several hundred miles to speak on a Sunday morning at a Friends' meeting. In some way I wanted to share in the quality of the religious experience upon which their whole spiritual encounter was projected. I made no preparation. I gave no thought to what I should say. No subject or text was selected. I sat with the leader of the meeting on the facing bench. We settled down into the quietness. Little by little, I became still within. That stillness merged with the stillness of the meeting. Then a very strange thing happened. There began turning up in my mind, words, words which were a part of a sentence. I had to wait for each word to be spelled out slowly and gradually. Finally the sentence spelled itself out. I read it! It formed a statement that had once come from the lips of Jesus. My mind seized upon it. I began wrestling with the idea that it gave me until it seemed that there was something within me that was ripe for expression. I moved my right foot back and my left foot just ahead and put my hands on the rail in front of me and was in the act of standing, when I heard behind me a woman's voice quoting that passage. She talked about it! All over the meeting, people arose, talking on the point, so that I began to wonder if I would have my chance at all. I had come many miles just to speak to these people. Only just before the hour was up, I had the opportunity to give my witness. During the waiting silence the traffic within me had stopped, the floodgate had opened, and there had begun to flow through me the spirit, the infinite resources of the living God.

The moment when this takes place becomes a sacramental moment, a moment that marks the step between the final act of meditation and the awareness of prayer. It is a moment when God appears. The waiting, the readying, the focusing, the centering down; then the spirit seems to pass over an invisible line of consciousness. The awareness of God bursts through all the corridors, all the reaches of the spirit.

I remember a rather interesting dramatization of this experience. Some of you may remember a play called *The Fool* in which the hero is the Christian. He has befriended a girl who is confined to a wheel chair. In one scene the girl in the wheel chair is on one side of the stage and on the other side, there is the "fool" himself along with a group of agitated workers. They accuse the fool of betraying their interests contrary to his profession and protestation. The leader of the group loses his temper, hits the fool on the chin, and knocks him down. When he falls, the crippled girl, who has never walked, gets out of her wheel chair, and *walks* across the stage. She kneels to help this man who has helped her and loved her. The leader of the group sees what has happened and cries: "Look, she walks! Down on your knees! God is in this room." It has been more than a quarter of a century since I saw this play in the theater. Even now as I relive it, I am caught up in the push of that moment, the sense of sacrament.

Less dramatic, but just as poignant and effective, is the experience of the individual, privately and personally, as he waits, readying his spirit in the quietness. The sacramental moment emerges within him. When it does, he prays. It may be that he prays for the first time in his life, because Something in him prays.

If I were to put into words what happened, it would be something like this: There is in every one of us an inward sea. In that sea there is an island; and on that island there is a temple. In that temple there is an altar; and on that altar burns a flame. Each one of us, whether we bow our knee at an altar external to ourselves or not, is committed to the journey that will lead him to the exploration of his inward sea, to locate his inward island, to find the temple, and to meet, at the altar in that temple, the God of his life. Before that altar, impurities of life are burned away; before that altar, all the deepest intent of your spirit stands naked and revealed; before that altar, you hear the voice of God, giving lift to your spirit, forgiveness for your sins, renewal for your commitment. As you leave that altar within your temple, on your island, in your inward sea, all the world becomes different and you know that, whatever awaits you, nothing that life can do will destroy you.

◆

O Sabbath rest by Galilee!
O calm of hills above,
Where Jesus knelt to share with Thee
The silence of eternity
Interpreted by love!

# 3. PRAYER AND PRESSURE

The Peace of God, which passeth all understanding, shall
guard my heart and thoughts.

There is the peace that comes when lowering clouds burst
and the whole landscape is drenched in rain,
refreshing and cool.

There is the peace that comes when gnawing hunger finds
intimate fulfillment in food,
nourishing and life-giving.

There is the peace that comes when hours of sleeplessness
are finally swallowed up in sleep,
deeply relaxing and calm.

There is a peace that comes when what has lurked so long
in the shadow of my mind stands out in the light,
I face it; call it by its name,
for better or for worse.

There is the peace that comes when sorrow is not relieved
When pain is not quieted
When tragedy remains tragedy, stark and literal
When failure continues through all the days
to be failure.

Is all this the peace of God?
Or is it the intimation of the peace of God?
The Peace of God shall guard my heart and thoughts.

There are feelings, untamed and unmanageable in my heart:
    The bitterness of a great hatred, not yet absorbed;
    The moving light of love, unrequited or unfulfilled,
    Casting its shafts down all the corridors of my days;
    The unnamed anxiety brought on by nothing in partic-
      ular,
    Some strange foreboding of coming disaster that does not
      yet appear;
    The overwhelming hunger for God that underscores all
      the ambitions, dreams and restlessness of my
      churning spirit.

Hold them, O peace of God, until Thy perfect work is in them
    fulfilled.

The Peace of God, which passeth all understanding, shall
    guard my heart and thoughts.

Into God's keeping do I yield my heart and thoughts, yea, my
    life—
With its strength and weakness
  Its failure and success,
  Its shame and its purity.

O Peace of God, settle over me and within me
So that I cannot tell mine from thine
And thine from mine.

### READING

Not once in a lifetime but again and again, and every day, and
perhaps many times a day, it must be encouraged to come, the
restoring sacrament of pause, and it comes not easily at first
without encouragement. Later it seeks one out.

It is the moment that corrects and counteracts our many
moments that become destructive to us, snatching us away, as
they do, breaking the divine accord.

For the sake of all things good and beautiful and true in him,
for the guarding of them in all his life, a man must seek again
that lifting instant in which he rouses his soul to repair the im-
paired harmony. Back to God he must call his thought, lift his
conscience to God for correction, bid his heart express again its
chosen loyalty to God. His whole self must make an effort to
re-set and re-establish and reconfirm itself in the life and love of
God.

They harassed thee, drove thee, Lord, twisted thy sayings
and hurt thy heart; they promised thee all things and for-
sook thee; they crowded upon thee that they might hear,
but listened without understanding, plagued thee with

*stupidities, injected barren meanings into thy so hopeful words, and foiled, and baulked, and darkened wisdom. And in those days of endangered vision, Lord, when men might have harmed thy spirit, when life might have disappointed thee and tamed the glory out of thee, in those days, it is said, thou didst lift up thy heart and pray.*

*"In those days" for him: in these days for me: days that try men's souls. And for us both the high and uplifted way of the spirit, lest the spirit die.*

—Oswald W. S. McCall

---

Prayer and pressure!

We are thinking of one of the very simple and natural expressions of the human spirit when it is exposed directly to the starkness, the intimate insistence of great need and tragedy. Prayer is for many of us the act of barnstorming the gates of heaven, wanting something for ourselves, desperately wanting something for someone else; turning to God in our extremity, as indeed we may, and are privileged to do. But always the point of reference is ourselves—our need for something that will relieve the pressure on us, for something that will make our lives easier, our way smoother, for something that will turn our darkness into light, that will lift the burden from our shoulders. Very often it seems as if we think of God as One who responds only to pressure that we exert upon Him out of our necessity. Evidently, we think that God cannot make up His mind; that He is in a state of indecision until we remind Him where we are in the universe and how great is our predicament. We call His attention to ourselves, and our needs, and our desperation. We even enlist the support of other people, that we may become an organized pressure group, to wrest from the stubborn

48

and recalcitrant hands of an arbitrary God that which He is withholding.

Two stories from the lips of Jesus have been used again and again in this connection. They have been lifted, perhaps out of the meaning which he had in mind, but let me sketch these two stories that we may hold them before us.

One is a story of a judge, who had no fear of man, no fear of God, no fear of fear. Apparently appointed for life, he was above the political process. A certain widow needed something desperately, something that this judge could give her. Every time he came to his outer chamber, there she was. When he would start home for his lunch, she walked a respectful distance behind him, stating her case. Everywhere he went, there she turned up; always saying the same thing, "Will you do this for me?" And finally, he relented and did it, not because he wanted to, not because he cared for her in her predicament, not because of any far-flung or intimate interpretation of the meaning of justice to which he was committed as a jurist. No. He did what the woman asked just because she kept worrying him, annoying him, harassing him; in order that he might have peace, he gave her peace.

The other story is that of a man who had unexpected visitors late one night. They were overnight visitors; and they were hungry. He didn't have any food to give them. Jesus says, he didn't have any bread. But he remembered that his neighbor next door might have some bread that he could borrow. He knocked at the door and the neighbor asked, "Who is it?" He identified himself, saying, "It is very late to call; everybody's gone to bed, I know. I didn't come for a social call, I want to borrow some bread."

"But I can't get up; I don't know if we have any food; besides I was just getting off to sleep after wrestling with insomnia for a long time. Now you come to disturb me. Go on back home like a good neighbor." He drifted off to sleep, but the knocking came again; he was called back into consciousness. On and on that went, until finally he got up. He gave bread to his neighbor, not because he loved him, not because he cared anything about the hungry visitors. He gave the bread finally because he wanted to go to sleep. Now the picture that comes to us is that God is like that, that God has to be convinced; that He can be convinced only if we give Him no ease, until at last we bend His will to meet our private demands. Pressure! Pressure! Pressure!

I think this says something about God that is unworthy; terribly unworthy! The point of the stories is not as is often indicated that God must be subjected to pressure in order to act on our behalf.

There is another kind of pressure which I think is more relevant and nearer to the real meaning of prayer. This is the pressure that human need makes upon us, which often is so unrelieved and intense in its character that we dare not present ourselves to God without including it. You remember a story that Jesus tells in this connection. Here was a man bed-ridden. His friends were deeply identified with him in his suffering and his need. They heard that Jesus was in the village and believed that he would minister to extreme need. So they thought that if this bed-ridden man could be brought into a face-to-face, primary, intimate exposure to, and encounter with, the love of Jesus, then a miracle would take place. The problem was how to get these two together. They went to the house where Jesus was and the house was packed with people standing in all the entrances. The yard, too, was crowded. There seemed no way that they could call their friend's need to Jesus' attention. Then they noticed that the roof wasn't so very high. If they worked together on it, they might jockey their friend up to the roof.

If they could tear away some of the thatched patches, they could let him down through the roof. All this they did and their friend was brought into direct contact with the love and the vitality of Jesus.

The meaning? I respond to the pressure of human need with such utterness that I cannot separate myself from the need. Therefore, I can never lay bare my own soul to the life, to the love, to the scrutiny, to the wisdom, to the judgment of God, without including in it others' needs that keep pulling at me.

I remember visiting a certain women's college whose dean I had known for many years. In the afternoon when I was at tea with her, I met her mother who was a lady about ninety years old. After the dean had to leave to go to a meeting, the mother said to me, "I'm very glad that my daughter has left, because I want to talk to you about something. I listened to what you had to say this morning in chapel, and I want to tell you something. I have been a member of a certain church for more than fifty-five years. We have a minister at that church now whom we do not love very much. As a matter of fact, he is not able to lead us and should have left long ago. He knows we feel that he should go, but he says that the Spirit of God tells him to stay; and he is going to stay, despite all our efforts. About a week ago, I decided I must do something about it. I took the entire afternoon off in my room. I began with the day I joined the church, more than a half-century ago, and unhurriedly, I reviewed my life in relation to the church; remembering all kinds of details, things that I hadn't thought of for years and years. I brought myself and the church up to the present moment and the present crisis. I went into detail, explaining to the Lord all about us, and about the minister, and then when I finished, I said, 'Now Lord, I have given you all the facts. Take them and do the best you can. I have no suggestions to make.'"

Pressure should not be put upon God. The right place for pressure is upon me, upon you, to bring my life, your life, in its totality, to an exposure to God. Not to give God orders. Not to presume that we are omniscient and can always understand what is best for us—tempting and natural as this is. We must ingather the fragments of our lives, the concerns of our spirits, the loves of our hearts—all of the aspects and dimensions of our living—we must ingather these and hold them in exposure to God. That is the ultimate responsibility of the human spirit. The Spirit of God, brooding over this stuff of our lives, will knead it and fashion it, infuse it with life, or withdraw vitality from some aspects of it. All of that is the divine prerogative. Our obligation is to make the exposure!

Now, this we cannot do unless we practice the habit of focusing our lives, somewhat according to the principle of recollection emphasized in historical Catholicism. There must be a conscious awareness of God in the shadow of our minds, day by day, as we handle our affairs, perform our tasks, fulfill our duties. All that we do must be referred to this point of awareness within us. We are not pursuing something esoteric and aesthetic.

We are developing the habit of holding in mind that our primary relationship and our primary loyalty, our ultimate commitment, is to God. The radical result of the conversion of the human spirit to God is that there is this riding point of referral that is always present in the things that we do, in the decisions that we make. It is in some ways like the thing that happens when a person has some kind of disease that he has to watch. He knows that he is perfectly normal in many ways; but he must never forget, in all of the details of his living, whatever the nature of his excitement and joy and enthusiasm—he must never forget that his heart isn't quite so strong as it was. Any constant awareness moves gradually to the center of consciousness until it becomes one with consciousness; thus all that I do and think and feel and delight in, ultimately stands or falls before the scrutiny, the judgment, and the love of God. Now if living moment by moment, day by day, as I go about my tasks and responsibilities, that is my pattern of behavior, then, when the time comes to enter the silent moment of prayer, there is merely a heightening of my experience. What I do in the moment of prayer is merely the creative synthesis of what I do always. And the pressure, the relentless pressure, is on me to live so that I desire to withhold nothing from Him—to let His life and His love and His scrutiny play over the stuff of my days. And that is enough. What He does with it, is not my affair!

———◆———

*O Love of God, Love of God, draw us in all the fragmentation of our splintered living, into the all-encompassing grasp of Thy Self. For us, this is enough. This is enough. Dismiss us with Thy Spirit, as Thou dost deal gently and tenderly with all the limitations of our structure and our living that we may not be alone in the way that we take, O God, our Father.*

# PART III

## CONCERNING GOD

◆ ▸ ◆

# 1. THE GOD OF LIFE

### MEDITATION

It is a commonplace remark that our lives are surrounded with so much movement, so many pressures, so many demands that our spirits are often crowded into a corner. As soon as we awaken in the morning we are taken over by the ruthlessness of our daily routine. Once out of bed, the timetable takes over. In some important ways this is good. It means that there is a regularity and a structure to our days that make it possible for us to accomplish tasks which would be impossible otherwise. So long as the daily routine is a tool in our hands with which we give expression to goals and purposes, all is well.

But there is another aspect to the matter of daily timetables—an oppressive aspect. We are made prisoner by timetables. We become busy—note the words—not, we are busy, but we become busy. Within ourselves we develop an inner sense of rush and haste. There is a kind of anxiety that is like the sense of impending doom that comes into the life when the spirit is crowded by too much movement.

It is true that for many people the demands upon their lives are so great that only careful planning in terms of a workable timetable can see them through. Even where the demands are not great and overwhelming, the economy, the efficiency of an established way of functioning, is undeniable. The purpose of such a pattern is not merely to accomplish more work and with dispatch but it is to increase the margin of one's self that is available for the cultivation of the inward parts. It takes time to cultivate the mind, it takes time to grow in wisdom, it takes time to savor the qualities of living, it takes time to feel one's way into one's self; it takes time to walk with God.

Forsake us not in the tempests of our daily activities, O, our Father, but tutor our minds and spirits in the great tranquillities, that deep within, we may be still and know that Thou art God.

### READING

God, I need Thee.
When morning crowds the night away
And tasks of waking seize my mind;
I need Thy poise.

God, I need Thee.
When love is hard to see
Amid the ugliness and slime,
I need Thy eyes.

God, I need Thee.
When clashes come with those

Who walk the way with me,
I need Thy smile.

God, I need Thee.
When the path to take before me lies,
I see it . . . courage flees—
I need Thy faith.

God, I need Thee.
When the day's work is done,
Tired, discouraged, wasted,
I need Thy rest.

————◆————

Even for those who are devout of spirit and consecrated of mind, the temptation to make a radical distinction between the God of Life and the God of Religion is one to which it is easy to succumb. Have you ever said, with reference to some recognized goodness, that it is true, that it is right, that it is ethical, that it is sound, but that it isn't practical; that it couldn't work; that it is not the way life is? When you make such a remark, you are saying that there is a distinction between the God of Life, on the one hand, and the God of Religion on the other.

The God of the whispered prayer, the God of the holy temple, the God of the muted music, the candlelight, the bended knee, the bowed head—the God of the holy place is One God. We recognize Him. We recognize that He holds command over our lives within the holy place. But out in the world away from the holy place, in the market place, in the stiff competition where men are struggling for mere survival, the ethical consideration is not primary. Is that what we say? At times when we are trying to get protection against the impersonal workings of the world of nature, trying to provide ourselves with shelter, and clothing, and warmth—then what about the moral demand? Or when we are trying to protect ourselves against the impersonal workings of the social order, needing to get some windbreak behind which we may take refuge and reproduce our kind and establish a basis for continuing security—what then about devotions to the God of our religious faith? In such struggles, does the God of Religion seem to be only an echo among the empty hills?

I am suggesting, however, that there is but One God, not two. I am saying that God is the God of Life, not merely the Creator of individual life, but the Creator of Life itself. When the human spirit undertakes to reach out for that kind of God, it is necessary and possible to assume that in the vastness of the universe there must be some kind of Mind, some kind of Control, some kind of all-comprehending Context, in which all living stuff finds meaning and point of reference.

When I was a boy in Florida, very often at night I would walk along the beach of the Atlantic Ocean. Dark night, bright stars. My little life so insignificant. I could sense not only the vastness of the universe, but the order of it. It sometimes seemed utterly impersonal, but I was aware of some vast order, some limitless and boundless structure of rationality. We know that, in our investigations of nature and science, whatever new fact we discover, whatever new thing may turn up on the horizon, it will fit into a comprehensive pattern, somewhere, sometime. So we work on the stuff of our experience over and over again.

For instance, here is a fact, a stubborn fact that does not seem to belong anywhere. We bring to bear upon that fact more and more resources of mind, drawing upon the gifts and the work and the knowledge of past generations, until at last this stubborn fact becomes domesticated in the universe. There seems to be, in the very nature of the human mind, the insistence that everything everywhere belongs. This sense of the wholeness in the universe gives us an immeasurable sense of security. And this is God, very God.

Now what about me as a person. I have a private world of hunger, of desires. I have dreams, aspirations. I want all the experiences that are beyond my control to become personalized so that I shall not be afraid to live. Whatever I encounter on my way must not dethrone my reason, and outrage my sense of worth. I must not seem to myself to be of no account. The vastness that holds in its hands the order of the universe, all these meanings that stretch beyond the furthest rim of human thought, must also include me and my little dream. The God of Life and the God of Religion must become, in me, One God, so that when I pray I do not seem to myself to be acting meaninglessly and irrationally.

If all this makes an ordered sense, then perhaps the God of Life has the same relationship to all His creatures that I have to all the raw materials that I am experiencing. Let me see if I can make that simpler. What do you mean when you say that you are you? What do you mean? If I ask any one of you, "Who are you?" you say, "I am I." "I am John." "I am Mary." "I am Suzie." What do you mean? Do you not mean that you are someone who is an experiencer of life and that all kinds of raw materials are going into you all the time? For instance, during this week you had a lot of experiences, raw material that you worked over and made into a part of you. So, if I want to know who you are, I will get what you have to say about yourself. But I will not stop there. I will find out also what your friends think of you, because that is a part of the impression, the impact that you have made upon living people. Their response to that impact is a part of the "youness" of you. I will also find out a little, if I can, of what people thought of you in the town where you grew up, what kind of boy they thought you were. I will want to know the things you did and the effect they had on you. Little by little, a picture will begin to emerge—a picture which is made up of you, the experiencer, as you have dealt with the raw materials that have gone into making you. As you grew older, these experiences and this picture became richer and richer. What you mean by yourself thus becomes more and more inclusive. All the time, at the center of your little world, you are trying to domesticate, trying to bring into meaning for you, the things that are happening to you. Now I think that that is like the relationship that God holds to the world. All the time He is bringing the raw material of life into some kind of order and pattern of wholeness and goodness and character. When I surrender my life to God, this process begins working in me.

The first thing that happens is some alteration in my behavior. It may be a slight alteration. The morning after I joined the church as a boy, I went fishing. The water was choppy and I lost an oar. Then I also lost my temper. Suddenly, as my temper followed the oar, I remembered that yesterday I had surrendered my life to God. Immediately, a new dimension of judgment moved into the whole context, and I found my temper being reduced a little; not much yet, but just a little. I had not consciously surrendered my right to a temper but almost mechanically, I had withdrawn my sanction to do this or this or this.

The second thing that happens is on a little deeper level. When I stabilize a change in behavior, when the change becomes routine, then it becomes a part of my habit structure, my habit pattern. This affects my character. Then a still deeper thing begins to happen. My consciousness is informed by the new behavior pattern. I now want to do the thing that I believe God wants me to do. I am not doing it for the sake of it—this is to operate on a more superficial level. I am not trying to emulate some example. I, at the center of myself, begin to *want* to do what, previously, I had thought that I *ought* to want to do. My desire to be what is the best and the truest and the highest moves *straight* from the center of *me* now rather than out of the book, or from out of any teaching or from out of the guidance that comes from something other than self-reference. A kind of spiritual autonomy begins to well up in me. What at one time I recognized as the Will of God operating in the world outside of me now becomes my will. Then, whatever are tragedies of my life, whatever involvement at any point whatsoever, there is this thing at work deep within. The God of the altar and the God of the market place become One God. Wherever I am, there is the stairway that leads from earth to heaven. Now to confess my sins and to offer my thanksgiving become one process. All my fear of life and of tomorrow dies, and even death becomes a little thing.

———◆———

*Teach us, our Father, that if we nourish within our minds and spirits those things that work against life, we shall spend our years stumbling in the darkness; that if we nourish within our minds and spirits those things that make for life, for wholeness, for truth, for love, we shall become like Thee. To become like Thee, O God, our Father, is the be-all and end-all of our desiring.*

# 2. THE LOVE OF GOD

## MEDITATION

God of our victory, answering our prayers with deeds of dread so loyally, all ends of the earth come to rely on Thee and distant shores. Thou by whose might the mountains are made firm and strongly fixed, by whom the roaring seas are stilled and the tumult of nations till dwellers at the world's far end are awed at the proofs of Thy power, and lands of sunrise and of sunset sing joyfully of Thee; Thou art good to the earth, giving water, enriching her greatly with rain from brimming streams divine. Thou providest the grain by preparing her duly, watering her furrows well, soaking her ridges, softening her with showers, and blessing all her growth. Thou art crowning the year with Thy goodness, rich stores drop where Thou passest. The very pastures of the downs overflow; the hills wear girdles of joy. The meadows are clothed with flocks; the valleys covered with corn, shouting and singing for joy. So I tell you, ask and the gift will be yours. Seek and you will find. Knock, and the door will open to you. For everyone who asks receives. The seeker finds. The door is opened to anyone who knocks. What father among you if asked by his son for a loaf will hand him a stone, or if asked for a fish, will hand him a serpent instead of a fish, or asked for an egg, will hand him a scorpion? Well, if for all your evil, you know to give your children what is good, how much more will your Father give the holy spirit from Heaven to those who ask Him. Think what a love the Father has for us in letting us be called children of God. And such we are. The world does not recognize us. That is simply because it does not recognize Him. We are children of God now. What we are to be is not apparent yet. But we do know that we shall be like Him. For we shall see Him as He is.

—Source Unknown

### READING

A Cincinnati paper says: "In a factory here there is a workman who had one small invalid child at home. He wrought at his trade with exemplary fidelity, being always in the shop at the opening of the day. He managed, however, to bear each evening to the bedside of his 'wee lad,' as he called him, a flower, a bit of ribbon, or a fragment of crimson glass—indeed, anything that would lie out on the white counter-pane and give color to the room. He was a quiet, unsentimental man, but never went home at night without something that would make the wan face light up with joy at his return. He never said to a living soul that he loved the boy so much. Still he went on patiently loving him, and by and by he moved that whole shop into positively real but unconscious fellowship with him. The workmen made curious little jars and cups upon their wheels, and painted diminutive pictures down their sides before they stuck them in the corners of the kiln at burning time. One brought some fruit in the bulge of his apron, and another engravings in a rude scrap-book. Not one of them whispered a word, for this solemn thing was not to be talked about. They put them in the old man's hat, where he found them; he understood all about it, and, believe it or not, cynics, as you will, but it is a fact that the entire pottery, full of men of rather coarse fiber by nature, grew quiet as the months drifted, becoming gentle and kind, and some dropped swearing as the weary look on the patient fellow-worker's face told them beyond mistake that the inevitable shadow was drawing nearer. Every day now someone did a piece of work for him and put it on the sanded plank to dry, so that he could come later and go earlier. So, when the bell tolled and the little coffin came out of the lonely door, right around the corner, out of sight, there stood a hundred stalwart workingmen from the pottery with their clean clothes on, most of whom gave a half day's time for the privilege of taking part in the simple procession and following to the grave that small burden of a child which probably not one had ever seen."

———◆———

It is not unusual for the preacher to attempt a learned theological discussion when addressing himself to such a theme as ours; he is tempted to take refuge in concepts that are a part of the reflective judgment of serious-minded men who have sought to reduce to manageable units of intellection, the meaning of the experience of the race with the adventure of love and tenderness, of graciousness and kindness. But instead of doing what I cannot do well, I should like you to think with me about the love of God at the level of your own experience and mine.

I have only one basic statement to make about the love of God and that is that it is always concerned with breaking the sense of isolation that the individual human spirit feels as it lives its way into life.

It is a truism to remark that we, all of us, feel the need for love. We want to be loved. We want to love. We want not merely to feel, but to know, that in whatever we are going through, or whatever we are experiencing, we are not alone. When we reflect upon this common need, this ordinary experience, we see several things: one is that we spend much time and energy as we live from day to day, trying to guarantee for ourselves the assurance that we are not alone, that we are not cut off. The little child does it when he seeks approval, when he does the thing that gives to his little self the assurance that he is being regarded. When he feels a great and exaggerated need for this attention, the child tends to stretch himself out of shape in a wide variety of ways. We adults say that he is "showing off." There is an inner need that is a permanent part of your life and my life, for belonging, for feeling and knowing and being assured that we are included in, as it were. We see it in many ways, even among people who by their attitudes and philosophies may regard themselves as completely indifferent to the mood, the need, the judgment, the outlook, the attitude of their fellows.

This need to be cared for, this need to be loved, expresses itself in our constant efforts to find someone in whose presence, and in relationship with whom, we shall feel understood, without necessity for pretending. You know how real this need is in your own life. How weary we are of managing always to get enough strength and vitality to be on our guard, to protect ourselves from the exposure of our lives to others' scrutiny. We knock at every door, hoping that we shall be able to have at least one experience in which we can let down our bars. We yearn not to have to pretend that we are better than we are, or worse than we are, but just to be. I want to be free enough within myself to be myself in the presence of some other person. Then, when we think of what such an experience does for us, we discover that love at the level of ordinary human experience confers upon the other person, the beloved, this freedom. I don't quite know how it is done; I'm not wise enough for that. The only thing I do know is that something happens to you when you become aware of another's love that releases you, that frees you. You relax even your need of privacy. You share the quality of your concern and your aspirations, your doubts, your limitations, with quiet confidence that whatever defects you reveal, the loved one will help you remove them from your life. The fault which you have covered up, lest its exposure give to another what could become, in his hands, an instrument of violence now becomes one of the creative means by which the quality and the integrity and the character of your life are improved and enriched.

If my child knows that I will forgive him, whatever he does, he may develop the technique that is called "I'm sorry." He knows that if he can excuse himself for his faults by saying "I'm sorry," then I am the one who is bound and nothing more need be done. This is to escape the personal responsibility of love.

A more adult aspect of the same reaction may be illustrated with the case of a person who violates the relationship between him and me. He knows that I will forgive and that I will say, "My forgiveness does not make it possible for you not to pay for this. I exact nothing from you and yet you will pay for it." This suggests that as life will provide retribution, I can afford to be indifferent to anything that my friend has done to me. As a matter of fact, that is not what happens. Even though I love you and do not wish to punish you, if you have injured me, there is some compensation for me in knowing, and seeing, that you must pay for your misdeeds. Actually, the knowledge that judgment will be visited upon us if we fail one another is an important element in our relationship. We want to feel that beneath our love is firmness, discipline, strength; that even if I excuse you, you cannot excuse yourself. Then judgment becomes self-judgment—the most searching and most bitter of all judgments.

Jesus as he began to think aloud of how the love of God operates, told the story about the prodigal son. The most important thing in the story is not so much the fact that the prodigal son was forgiven by his father, though that is important and crucial, and very exciting and wonderful, and very redemptive. But the thing that I see in it always is that the boy had to purify himself by his self-judgment because of the way in which he had violated the relationship between him and his father. His father forgave him, but how could he forgive himself? He had to find ways by which he could redeem his life from the lacerations inflicted upon it by his own willfullness. Meanwhile, the creative attitude of his father's love held firm the context, the climate, the atmosphere, in which the boy could work out his salvation.

It seems to me that this points up an important thing about the love of God. In the religious experience, the individual finds fulfilled what he has glimpsed in his other experiences of love: namely, that in the presence of his God he becomes aware of being dealt with totally. Whether he is a good person or a bad person, he is being dealt with at a point beyond all that is limiting, and all that is creative, in him. He is dealt with at the core of his being, and at that core he is touched and released. With insight, with wisdom, with patience, with courage, with devotion, with commitment, he can now deal with the facts of his own life; and he will seek to introduce all these qualities into his relationships with his fellows.

In quietness, in prayer, I become aware of the meaning of the love of God. I may see it or find it as I discover the world of nature, as I observe the pattern of life-behavior around me. I may see descriptive pictures of what seems to me the manifestation of the love of God as I watch this expression in personality, or that expression in personality. I look over the whole stretch of human history and see movements toward creativity and redemption and, central to it all, the redemptive love of Jesus. But the moment when I discover the meaning of the love of God is not in the context of a million minor coincidences, but in the moment when I, as a human being, am able to experience the sense of being completely and totally understood in the Presence of God. This bottoms all the adventure of my life. This is the ultimate immunity against isolation. This is the only bulwark against the stark devastation of affliction. No argument, no series of "for instances" in my own life, no aspects of my behavior pattern, are as important as this. I must know for myself that I am not alone; that in the solitariness of my own existence, when I am stripped to whatever is in me that is literal and irreducible—that here, in that ultimate outreach of my spirit, I am understood.

This is after all what the work of the psychiatrist and the psychoanalyst and the counselor is about—all of these people who are dealing with the tempest-tossed and the broken; this is what they are getting at. Somehow the individual has to have at his core a sense of communal confirmation, a sense of being cared for at a point in him that is beyond all the turmoil in his mind, the wickedness of his deeds, the struggling effort toward goodness and decency. Jesus said, "Look how the lilies of the field grow; they neither toil nor spin, and yet, I tell you, even Solomon in all his grandeur was never robed like one of them." Jesus was talking about this same idea that a man may have at the core a sense of being sustained, confirmed, not cut off. Whoever is the creative vehicle for exposing the human spirit to this great possibility becomes at once Savior and Redeemer, for he puts within reach of the soul that which gives a man an ultimate immunity against the terrifying ravages of isolation. When I speak of the love of God, I speak finally of the whisper in the heart that gives this assurance. Anything else, however important and relevant it may be, turns on whether or not you, I, have this kind of assurance.

———◆———

*How little, O God, we trust in Thee. Forgive the weakness and the feebleness of our minds and our spirits. Accept, O God, the joy of our hearts for the light that breaks in us when we have heard Thy whisper. Dismiss us with Thy spirit, and grant unto us Thy peace, our Father.*

# 3. THE GRACE OF GOD

## MEDITATIONS

"And man without God is a seed upon the wind." A sure and searching word from a sensitive, contemporary figure. What a picture! A tiny living thing awaiting its moment of fulfillment, caught up in the movement of tremendous energy, at the mercy of forces that are not responsive to its own ends! There is a grand unconscious vitality unfolding with mounting energy its vast impersonal purpose. In the grip of something like this, what is a tiny seed—no more than a particle of dust, a nameless nothing. Here is the abandonment of all purpose, the stark helplessness of that without mooring or anchor. The fact that there is locked up within the seed a private world of pattern and design makes no difference to the fierce velocities that sweep it on their reckless, relentless way.

"Man without God is a seed upon the wind." He is a victim of the currents of life that carry him where they will with a bland unmindfulness of purposes and ends which belong to him as a living, thinking, feeling creature. It means that such a man has no sense of center—he takes his clue to all meaning and values from the passing moment, the transitory event, the immediate issue of his day. He is at home nowhere because he is not at home "somewhere." The master speaks of this in his searching question, "What would a man give in exchange for his soul?"

But there is a sense in which a man with God is a seed upon the wind—the man who has made the primary surrender, the commitment, the yielding to God at the core of his being. He is one who has relaxed his will to exercise and hold firm the initiative over his own life. This does not come without exacting struggle of the soul. One by one the outposts of his spirit are captured, retaken, and lost again through hours, months, even years of warfare, until at last the very citadel of his spirit is under siege and he is subjected to an utter yielding. There follows often the long silence when nothing stirs. Then out of the vast quiet of his vanquished spirit something stirs and a new life emerges that belongs more to God than to self. The movement now rests with Purposes that are beyond the little purposes, with Ends that transcend the private ends as the Purposes and Ends of God. Yes, there is a sense in which a man with God is a seed upon the wind.

> Life, you have beaten me, still,
> With stinging wounds, I kiss your hands,
> Though you have tortured me until
> My joy was crushed, my hopes, my will
> For things I do not understand.

Though I have trembled at your power
And wept in terror, hour by hour;
For all our struggling, hate and strife,
I love you, Life.
Though what I build, you will destroy;
Though what I seek and hoard, you take;
Though you have snatched joy after joy
From my weak hands, and, though you break
My heart, and all my dreams dispel,
And silence every drum and fife
That makes my march less terrible . . . .
I love you, Life.
And, Life, for all your cruel powers,
For all your proud brutality;
How wonderful the few brief hours,
When you are kind to me.

—J.F.B., State Prison of Massachusetts

### READING

The quality of mercy is not strain'd;
It droppeth as the gentle rain from heaven
Upon the place beneath: it is twice bless'd;
It blesseth him that gives and him that takes:
'Tis mightiest in the mightiest; it becomes
The thronèd monarch better than his crown;
His sceptre shows the force of temporal power,
The attribute to awe and majesty,
Wherein doth sit the dread and fear of kings;
But mercy is above this sceptred sway,
It is enthroned in the hearts of kings,
It is an attribute to God himself,

*And earthly power doth then show likest God's*
*When mercy seasons justice.*
— SHAKESPEARE, *The Merchant of Venice*

———◆———

The Grace of God. The word "grace" came originally from a Latin word meaning "pleasing," and the first definition given it in modern dictionaries still makes it applicable primarily to physical form or manner. We speak of a person who moves with grace; with an extra something that makes the difference between awkwardness and beauty. It is an extra quality, not apparently indigenous in the person, or in the thing, but that fits into it as a benediction and heightens its meaning. You find the grace note in music, the funny little note that hangs around the bar and gives a little extra something to the music. Here is a rather crude illustration of this extra something: Many years ago a man wrote a popular song called "My Wife Has Gone to the Country." It fell flat; no one liked it. Then another song writer heard the song and did something to it. He added a word, and the word was "Hooray!" Then the song simply swept the country.

We see grace most effectively and simply expressed in an ordinary act of human kindness. Have you ever been kind to anyone? Really kind? Or have you been on the receiving end of an act of kindness? We say that a man is "worthy of honor" because he has pursued some end that has brought a great benediction and blessing upon his generation or his age. We say that a man is "worthy of respect" not only because of the way he deports himself, but also because he is a child of God, and in him is the breath of life. All of this makes sense. But when we say that a man is "kind," we are talking about something that transcends all obligations, all necessities. The kind act is one

73

in which the individual bestows upon another human being something that in a thousand years the other human being could not really merit. When someone is kind to you, you can never repay the favor because you can't truly say: "This kindness that has been bestowed upon me is one that I deserve; therefore I can measure it and pay it back."

When Oscar Wilde was being brought from the court of bankruptcy to the jail, handcuffed to the sheriff, the corridor was crowded with milling, jeering people. One little man walked out from the midst of the crowd, took off his hat, stood at attention, and bowed his head while the prisoner and the sheriff passed. A simple gratuitous act. Oscar Wilde, writing about it, said, "This I can never repay." The spontaneous expression of an additional quality, an extra something, had made the desert of his prison blossom like the rose.

Now, the grace of God has that quality. It seems to be inherent in the structure of life itself, life's capacity to be self-healing; the private individual's life seems always to impinge upon a broader dimension that affects his life and seems to invade it from the outside, moving in to make changes here and there.

Let me illustrate this. I heard Dr. Richard Cabot many years ago give a lecture on the wisdom of the body. He said that when he was on the outpatient ward of a hospital in Boston, a patient died following a very bad accident. He was a man about seventy years old and his wife, grieving over him, said, "Think of it. I have known him since we were little children four or five years old and he has never been sick a day in his life." Dr. Cabot said he had always wanted to perform an autopsy on a man who had never been sick. He talked with the wife and she agreed to let him do it. When he performed the autopsy, he discovered some very surprising things. He discovered, for instance, that the man had had tuberculosis for a long time

74

but that nature had so built walls around the tubercle bacilli that they leaked no poison into the bloodstream. The man was a bartender. He didn't drink. But, for forty-five years he had been a taster, with the result that his liver had been affected. Here, too, the wisdom of the body had brought about such functional changes that the man had no knowledge of anything wrong. Dr. Cabot described various other discoveries, all illustrating that inherent in the life process there is moving a creative, redemptive element which belongs to life itself. Yet it seems to operate according to principles that are independent of logic and of rational order.

Another illustration: Some years ago I was crossing the United States by the southern route. I had been advised to stop at San Antonio to see the Alamo. So, when the train stopped at noon for a half hour, I got off to look around. If I found myself interested, I could stay till the next train. At first, I thought I would not stay, but just as the conductor announced that the train was ready to go, in a split second I changed my mind. I ran into the car, took my topcoat and bag, and jumped off the slowly moving train, much to the consternation of the conductor. I caught the midnight train. The next day when the train to which I had transferred approached Yuma, Arizona, it slowed. Just off the track ahead were two huge engines like two monsters that had been in a life-and-death struggle, and some fifteen or twenty steel cars twisted and turned over. Their sides had been cut open by acetylene torches so that the dead could be removed. That was the train that I had suddenly jumped off, several hours before.

This may be a poor example of what I mean, but certainly the grace of God operates in such a way that the individual life —your life and my life—seems constantly to be the recipient of something that does not arise within its own personal pattern.

A second dimension of grace must be given some comment. The Christian doctrine gives a special meaning to the concept of grace. It is this: that God initiates in the human spirit desires, longings, hungers, which when fulfilled, make us whole. When we resist then we stay the movement of the redemptive grace of God. We relax into them, accept them, are guided by them; we discover that God in us is calling to the God of Life. Every kind act, every tender movement of the heart, every gracious deed, becomes a sacrament of the living God. Christian theology, recognizing this universal human experience, teaches that the crowning, dramatic expression of the grace of God is manifest in the giving of the only Son of God as the living sacrifice for all men. Whatever may be a man's feeling about the validity of this doctrine, it is rooted in the experience of life that is as universal as is the quivering response of joy when a life has been touched by a kind act, a loving deed. I become like Him, when I respond to His movement in me.

———◆———

*What in us is of low estate, raise and support. Give unto our lives, O God, our Father, all that we need to make us living instruments in Thy hands. Grant that Thy peace and Thy grace may be with us as we go our way, and our lives may joy Thy heart and delight Thy Spirit.*

# 4. JUSTICE AND MERCY

## MEDITATION

The Great Silence that surrounds us as we together share the spirit and the love of God throws us back upon ourselves, deepening our insights into the meaning of our own lives; revealing to us in the quietness, the lights and the shadows of our days; defining for us the significance of our deeds during the past week; opening for us the doors of truth and understanding, that we refuse to enter on Monday, Tuesday, Wednesday, Thursday, Friday, or Saturday. We remember the hurried word uttered in a moment of irritation or anxiety, a word which we could not recall, but watched with bated breath as its fearful consequences unfolded before our eyes in the life of another. In the quietness, we see more clearly the meaning of some of the larger events by which our common life is surrounded, events having to do with the fates of nations and peoples, events having to do with the future peace and health of the world. All of these things move before our view as we sit in the midst of the congregation but each in his own isolation enveloped by the stillness, the quiet, the Presence of God. We ask no dream, no prophet ecstasy, no sudden rending of the veil of clay, but take the dimness of our souls away while there is still time. For us, O God, our Father, this is enough. This is enough for us.

## READINGS

I dreamt God took my soul to Hell.

To my right among the trees were men working. And I said to God, "I should like to go and work with them. Hell must be a very fruitful place, the grass is so green."

God said, "Nothing grows in the garden they are making."

We stood looking; and I saw them working among the bushes, digging holes, but in them they set nothing; and when they had covered them with sticks and earth each went a way off and sat behind the bushes watching; and I noticed that as each walked he set his foot down carefully looking where he trod. I said to God, "What are they doing?"

God said, "Making pitfalls into which their fellows may sink."

I said to God, "Why do they do it?"

God said, "Because each thinks that when his brother falls he will rise."

I said to God, "How will he rise?"

God said, "He will not rise."

And I saw their eyes gleam from behind the bushes.

I said to God, "Are these men sane?"

God said, "They are not sane; there is no sane man in Hell."

—OLIVE SCHREINER

*I have never caused anyone to weep;*
*I have never spoken with a haughty voice;*
*I have never made anyone afraid;*
*I have never been deaf to words of justice and truth.*
—*The Egyptian Book of the Dead*

◆

"Vengeance is mine, I will repay."
And again, "The Lord will judge
his people."
Hebrews 10:30

Blessed are the merciful, for they
shall obtain mercy.
Matthew 5:7

Justice, according to America's first and pioneer sociologist, Lester Ward, is defined as the artificial equalization of unequals —the restoration of balance, of equilibrium, in a situation in which the balance has been upset. No question is raised about the fundamental character of the status quo that is re-established. Such justice is represented by the figure that has come down to us from another period—the blindfolded woman with the scales in her hand. The blindfold is there to indicate that justice should not be influenced by any considerations that might sway the emotions.

Not many years ago a federal judge of a certain district in South Carolina, with this conception of justice, was called upon to make a ruling upon the legal rights of suffrage as these rights were being interpreted in the Democratic primary in South Carolina. He arrived at a decision according to his interpretation of the application of the Jeffersonian doctrine of democracy. He felt no responsibility for the consequences of his ruling. He detached himself from his background of life and thought and training and conditioning. He merely interpreted the law. Then he discovered that his conclusion did violence to his own culture pattern. He found himself in the midst of great emotional turmoil, with consequences so devastating that finally he left his native state to establish residence elsewhere.

The mention of the word "justice" may send our minds hurtling over a wide variety of comparable incidents, but they are of no concern for our immediate purpose. I want us to think about the meaning of justice and mercy in terms of our own innermost sense, not merely of statutory rightness, but of the significance of life and existence and the meaning of God.

There are two basic approaches to justice that we might explore. Men appeal to justice when they are dealing with one another from within a context of equality of will, and when neither has the power to inflict his will upon the other. In the stalemate, justice is appealed to as that which is outside the context. This is the justice of the court of law and I need not illustrate it.

There is another sense in which men appeal to justice, and this is in line with my present thinking. We may be so placed that we have power, legitimate power, over another human being. If we relax that power, we establish within ourselves a voluntary distance, between the expression of our power and ourselves. Let's talk about that. You do it with your children, don't you? Every parent has power over his child up to a certain point. He may exercise that power or refrain from doing so. One incident occurs to me now in which I was not willing to establish voluntary distance, but stood on my parental constitutional grounds.

One day I was reading something which I had to finish before going out of the house. My four-year-old daughter came rushing in, saying, "Daddy, here's something that I want you to do for me right now, please!" And I said, "But I can't do that now. You see I'm reading this book and I have to finish it before a certain time." That made no impression. She insisted. Then I repeated what I had said, putting a rumble in my voice that surrounded her with a certain atmosphere of insecurity. She bristled, and stood her ground; then finally in disgust she went out of the room with her will untouched by mine.

Jesus talks about justice; do you remember? "Ye have been told, 'An eye for an eye, a tooth for a tooth' "! That was some advance over a still earlier justice that argued that if a man injures me, there is only one limitation that I should recognize in inflicting injury upon him: my strength or perhaps his endurance. The justice to which Jesus referred said that if a man put my eye out, I had the right to put his eye out. The measure of what I might inflict upon him was determined beforehand by the measure of what he had inflicted upon me. Jesus suggested that there is something different to be done. When a man inflicts an injury upon me, I must establish voluntary distance from him, between what I might do to him, and what I actually *do* to him.

This is what the psalmist and other men of religious insight insist upon as the basis of the relationship between God and man. God introduces into His relationship with men this voluntary distance between what He is able to do, or between what seems to be the logical result of a deed, and what He wills to do in the situation. "He hath not dealt with us after our sins, nor rewarded us according to our iniquities."

Let us see what this means in terms of mercy.

A. Blindfolded justice is appealed to in a situation of practical equality in which there is a power stalemate. It becomes a kind of referee that makes a decision on considerations that have nothing to do with power, extenuating circumstances, or the like. Mercy does not appear in this picture at all.

B. Justice is appealed to when individuals are in situations that are unequal in terms of the power which they are able to exercise. If the man with the power imposes his will upon the other, a very curious thing happens. He strips the other person of that precious ingredient of his personality that gives him a private autonomous existence; he reduces him to a mere thing. Or if you, having such power, refrain from exercising it, then you permit the other's integrity of will, of mind, of personality, to remain intact, regardless of what might be considered his just deserts. You have voluntarily established within yourself a distance between your power and your will.

The merciful act, then, is the act of an individual who is willing to refrain from the exercise of the logic of his power over another and recognizes a principle that transcends the power relationship. Mercy is what the second person experiences when he realizes that he could have been victimized, but was not. His response for being spared is gratitude, not so much gratitude to the person who spared him, as to this principle, the quality in human life, that prompts one man to withhold the fulfillment of his will because of considerations that transcend for him the necessity to fulfill his will.

You remember how Jesus dealt with a situation of this sort. There was a servant who owed his master a lot of money; so he went to his master and said, "Times are pretty difficult, and I wish you would do something about this. You can throw me into jail, but be kind to me." And the creditor settled the matter in a way that was creative and redemptive, relieved the servant of the obligation. The man went away rejoicing. Then as he was walking down the street, full of the elixir of this

82

wonderful feeling of relief, he saw a man that owed money to him and he said, "I want to see you—what about the money you owe me?" And the second man said, "Times are difficult, you know that."

"That has nothing to do with it. You are under obligation to pay me. The time is up. I want my money, or you take the consequences."

The servant had been grateful to his master for excusing him, but he did not have the added grace to pass on to another the mercy that had been shown him. If he had loved justice, he might have sought within himself the quality that he had seen in its glory in the deed that had blessed his life.

What does all of this mean, then, to you and to me? In how many of your relationships—intimate, primary, personal relationships—does your power, of whatever character, place another human being at your mercy? Are you so full of pride, arrogance, and personal insecurity as a human being that you dare not run the risk of establishing within yourself voluntary distance between your power and the exercise of it? If you do establish this distance, then at once you begin to participate in a dimension of living and experiencing, in a dimension of reality that lifts you into the category of an authentic child of God. More and more, in the very core of your being, you feel yourself to be of infinite worth and significance in the presence of God. You recognize, honor, this quality in Him by dealing with His fellows out of the stirring vitality of this inner awareness.

One more thing. Obviously there are all sorts of fringes that cannot be touched upon briefly, but the underlying principle should be gripped because then we can work on it for days and days, and months and years, for the rest of our lives. There is at bottom, beneath the whole structure of justice and mercy, the integrity of the moral order. In any moral order there is an inherent and inevitable relationship between the deed and the consequence. The degree to which I am willing to take my position on the moral integrity of life, to that degree am I willing to affirm in my daily life that the evil deed does not go unpunished. But I am not the avenger! My responsibility is to keep alive the margin between the exercise of whatever power may be mine and what I know I should want if the situation were reversed. I am merciful when I become the kind of sensitive human being who keeps this distance between the ruthless application of his will upon another human being, and what he does. Then the strength of God becomes available to me in terms of insight, in terms of endurance, in terms of strength of spirit, in terms of a benediction of His grace. Justice becomes Mercy. Mercy fulfills Justice.

———◆———

O God, our Father, all the confusion inspired by our weakness and our inadequacy and our failure we make as a part of our offering to Thee. What in us is dark, illumine. What is low, raise and support; that, in ways that we can understand, and in ways that transcend the limitations of our understanding, we may be living instruments in Thy hands. Do not let us separate from Thy Spirit, as we separate one from the other, but go with us, O God, go with us, our Father.

# PART IV

## CONCERNING PEACE

———— ◆ ————

# 1. PEACE IN OUR LIVES

### MEDITATION

*I make of my life an offering to God.*

*Fierce indeed is the grip by which we hold on to our lives as our private possession. The struggle to achieve some sense of individuality in the midst of other people and other things is grim. Always we are surrounded by persons, forces, and objects which lay siege to us and seek to make of us means to their ends or at least to their fulfillment. The demand is ever present to distinguish between the self and the not-self.*

*There are moments of enthusiasm when with mounting excitement we absorb ourselves in something beyond ourselves. When this happens we fight at length to get back home, to come again into the familiar place, to be secure in our own* boundaries. Again and again the process repeats itself, wearing down the walls that shut us in.

Of course, a man may by early resolution, by frustration, by bitter experience withdraw more and more from all involvements. By this process he seeks to immunize himself against hurts and from what seems to be certain disaster. Behold such a man. His spirit shrinks, his mind becomes ingrown, his imagination inward turning. The wall surrounding him becomes so thick that deep within he is threatened with isolation. This is the threat of death. Sometimes his spirit breaks out in reverse by giving voices to inward impulses, thus establishing by the sheer will to survival a therapy for the corrosion of his spirit.

For all of this religion has a searching word. "Deep within are the issues of life." "The rule of God is within." "If thou hadst known the things which belong unto thy peace." There is a surrender of the life that redeems, purifies, and makes whole. Every surrender to a particular person, event, circumstance, or activity is but a token surrender, the temporary settling of the life in security. These are not to be ignored but they are all passing and transitory. They end in tightening the wall of isolation around the spirit. They are too narrow, too limited, finally unworthy.

The surrender must be to something big enough to absolve one from the little way, the meager demand. There can be no tranquillity for the spirit unless it has found something about which to be tranquil. The need for a sense of peace beyond all conflict can only be met by something that gathers up into itself all meaning and all value. It is the claim of religion that this is only found in God. The pathways may vary but the goal is one.

Nevertheless, I thank Thee, Lord, for nests.

I thank Thee, Lord, for places of sweet comfort and security, without which, as nestless birds out of their shells but not yet into their feathers, we should have perished.

I thank Thee for defenses and seclusions, for nooks where there is peace and harbors where the wind does not come.

I thank Thee for protecting arms and for protecting minds that have wrought for us and thought for us and planned and made provision.

I thank Thee that we have not always had to shape decisions for ourselves, that some have risen to shield us from the fierce brunt, that if the outer world is cruel we have been saved from knowing it, that for us so much kindly velvet has made hard places soft.

I thank Thee, Lord, for nests, for their brave, resistant ramparts and their gentle, downy ease.

Many tender and young things in us could never have waxed and grown, but would have died like buds in a frost, if they had had no shelter.

Many good and beautiful things in us, had they been pitched untimely into the world, would have drowned like puppies thrown into deep water.

In a world where soon or later we must meet treachery, selfishness, and exploitation, I thank Thee for years of incubation, nursing, and defending, during which the good in us was nourished and confirmed.

For home that cared enough to keep doors shut;

For faith that had a better air to breathe than cynicism and denial;

For all postponements of strokes that might have come too soon, all walls against blasts that babes could not endure;

For fairy ignorances, rose-pink illusions, stare-eyed hope and peace and joy,

Yea, for nests,

I thank Thee, Lord!

—OSWALD W. S. McCALL

———◆———

One of the fruits of the spirit about which the apostle Paul writes is peace. When we hear the word "peace" our minds turn first to those expectations of our common aspirations, collective hopes, and fears which have to do with the nations of the earth, including our own. At such moments, we dream of the fulfillment of the prophecy that men will beat their swords into ploughshares and their spears into pruning hooks. It is well that we should think and dream in this way.

I am thinking now, however, about peace in a more intimate and personal dimension. I am thinking of peace in terms of the strivings and realities of our private worlds. For instance, there is the peace of innocence. The lines quoted from McCall have to do with that kind of peace. This is the peace that is described in the story of the creation of man and his life in the Garden of Eden. Sometimes, from the heights of our sophistication and knowledge, we regard such peace as very naïve; we look upon innocence with condescension and studied arrogance.

But the peace of innocence serves a fundamental purpose in human experience. It is not accidental, it is not due merely to undernourishment that children who have never had the opportunity to be children seem to make up the rank and file of the so-called delinquents. Apparently such children have a nervous system and a body that is angry. With what approximates blindness, they strike against all manifestations of authority. I think that this is true because the growing child needs all its inner creative resources to lay a sound and orderly foundation of bodily and nervous functioning against the stresses and strains of the maturing years. Innocence makes that possible. This is the period of the windbreak behind which the quiet inner process may build, grow, deepen, and provide for the long pull of the later years. If there is no windbreak, if the child does not have the privilege of innocence but must start off in life as if he is mature, must meet all of the difficulties that go with the struggles of adulthood, then the creative and redemptive work of childhood is defeated. How fortunate is the human being whose life has been blessed with the privilege of the innocence of childhood!

This necessity for innocence works in another way, too. The dream of innocence is a part of the prologue to all of the developed cultures and religions of the world. The dream of the idyllic moment, when everything was perfect and there were no tensions, is the dream of the Garden of Eden. Suppose the human spirit did not have this quality in its myths of creation. Think of it! It is true that innocence is lost because of sin, error, disobedience. However, the creative and effective vitality of the dream of innocence never deserts the horizon of man. This is of breathless significance. It says that in the midst of all the contradictions of experience, in the midst of all the tensions of life, the possibility always remains that one may recapture in fact the quality of the idyllic moment inherent in the myth. Here is provided a steadying source of authority and inspiration. I thank

God for the peace of innocence as caught and preserved in the myth. Without it life would be stark and barren indeed.

Then there is the peace of exhaustion. In the old part of Rock Creek Cemetery in Washington, D.C., there is a statue done by St. Gaudens. It was erected over the grave of the wife of Henry Adams. The figure of a woman is seated in a huge chair at the center of a crescent-shaped marble bench. The whole body is draped in a tremendous piece of bronze which ends in a cowl over her head, leaving only her face exposed. The elbow is resting on the arm of her chair, and her face is supported by her fingers and thumb. The look is straight ahead. There is no manifestation of any emotion in her face; one is struck by the fact that her countenance is devoid of any recognizable qualities. It is as if the eyes have cried themselves out so that there are no more tears left. She has moved beyond all temptations and all tensions and has been exhausted by living. Such is the peace of exhaustion! Have you ever experienced it? Have you ever felt that the experience through which you have passed has drained you of everything so that there is nothing left? There are times when a human being may be so hurt and cast down to such a depth that he cannot be hurt any more. This is exhaustion that has some of the quality of—but minus the dynamics of —the stillness of absolute motion.

When I was a boy, I heard a minister preach a sermon about heaven and hell. I shall always remember it, particularly what he said about hell. He described what people were doing there and, of course, he gave full attention to the sins of his own community. One such sin was dancing! He told that he came to a great ballroom full of people dancing. They were couples. The unique thing about what they were doing is this: None of them could stop dancing. Their faces were the faces of exhaustion. But they had to dance for ever and ever and ever. And each with the same partner! His thesis was that the thing, the doing of which sent you to hell, was the thing that you had to do throughout eternity. It was this that made it hell. Here is exhaustion, but exhaustion floated by muted vitality.

Finally, there is the peace of endurance and triumph. This is the quality about which we think when we reflect upon the ultimate significance of faith in human life and human struggle. William W. Story in "Io Victis" puts it this way:

> I sing the hymn of the conquered,
> who fell in the Battle of Life,—
> The hymn of the wounded, the beaten,
> who died overwhelmed in the strife;
> Not the jubilant song of the victors,
> for whom the resounding acclaim
> Of nations was lifted in chorus,
> whose brows wore the chaplet of fame,
> But the hymn of the low and the humble,
> the weary, the broken in heart,
> Who strove and who failed, acting bravely
> a silent and desperate part;
> Whose youth bore no flower on its branches,
> whose hopes burned in ashes away.
> From whose hands slipped the prize they had grasped at,
> who stood at the dying of day
> With the wreck of their life all around them,
> unpitied, unheeded, alone,
> With Death swooping down o'er their failure,
> and all but their faith overthrown.

It is the margin of faith that remains which turns endurance into triumph.

There is a radical difference between this kind of peace and the peace of innocence. Goodness and innocence are not synonymous. One does not think of a little child as being good; a little child is innocent, not good. We say that a man is good as to this or that in particular when he has learned how to distill peace out of chaos; when he has learned how to brood over the ugliness of his experience until at last out of its churning depth, beauty itself emerges. Such a person is good as to that kind of triumphant achievement. He knows that the peace of triumph is in a profound sense the peace of God that passes all human understanding. It passes all human understanding because of an essential paradox. There seems to be inherent in it a profound contradiction. A great American philosopher makes the same observation. He says that one can understand the peace that comes when, after great loneliness, one finds a friend, or after great hunger, one finds food to eat; or after long illness, one finds strength and vitality with returning health. All that makes sense. We can understand the gratitude that pervades the spirit, and perhaps the body, when one experiences peace of that kind. But the peace that is the peace of God that passeth all understanding comes when the struggle of life is not relieved. There are times when I have no choice but to settle down with the thing that is my predicament and know that I have no option available to me but to deal with it; for better or for worse —this is my battle. I could wish that it were otherwise. I could wish for some miracle that would suddenly release me, but there is no miracle. I must deal with my struggle, my problem, my battle, my tragedy. I cannot escape.

Now, the peace that comes when the struggle is not relieved; the peace that comes when the pain is not abated is my personal discovery. I have stretched the length and breadth of my spirit until at last I squeeze from its stubborn, recalcitrant, and often violent churnings, tranquillity. No man can be tranquil until he has discovered that about which to be tranquil. The peace that comes when pain is not relieved is the peace that comes "shimmering on the crest of a wave of pain. It is the spear of frustration transformed into a shaft of light." Such is the peace of God that passeth all human understanding. Whenever it emerges in human experience, whenever it is the personal discovery of the individual, we see one who knows that he can abide, who can stand anything that life can do to him, who never gives up. He knows the peace of God.

There is the peace of innocence, the peace of exhaustion, the peace of endurance and triumph. But the greatest of these is the peace of endurance and triumph. May that peace of God be yours for ever and ever.

# 2. NOT PEACE—A SWORD—I

## MEDITATION

"In the year that King Uzziah died
   I saw the Lord."

Thus speaks the prophet out of the despair of heart
By which all his waking hours were surrounded.

For a long time, the roots of which lay buried deep within
   the struggles of the past,
The prophet felt the mounting pressure of his empty
   years. . . .
Then came tragic tidings! Sadness leaped from voice to
   voice;
"Uzziah is dead! King Uzziah is dead."
     The wasting flesh; the living death; the silent seeping
      of vital strength until at last

Leprosy worked its perfect work.
Such was the fate of the king.
Blind with grief—the prophet sought solace in the place
  where in all his weary years
His father, his father's father and those before,
Had sought and found the strength to go yet another day.
Here he laid bare the agony of his loss
Until at last, before his dreary eyes, there burst
The vision bright, so vast that all the earth was filled with
  its glory.
Here was the Great Disclosure,
Always old, always new:
Tears of mourning to
Tears of rejoicing;
Hours of anguish to
Hours of soaring;
Darkness exhausting itself in light;
Sorrow emptying itself in joy.

"In the year that King Uzziah died
I saw the Lord."

Thus speaks the prophet out of the despair of heart
By which all his waking hours were surrounded.

### READINGS

Go Thy way, all things say,
Thou hast thy way to go, thou hast thy day
To live; Thou hast thy need of thee to make
In the hearts of others; do thy thing; yes awake
The world's great thirst for yet another man!

And be thou sure of this; no other can
Do for thee that appointed thee of God;
Nor any light shall shine upon thy road
For other eyes;
    Thee the angel calls,
As he calls others; and thy life to thee
Is precious as the greatest's life can be
To him; so live thy life and go thy way.
                —RICHARD WATSON DIXON

     Take no thought for your life,
         what ye shall eat,
         or what ye shall drink;

     Nor yet for your body,
         what ye shall put on.

     Is not the life more than meat,
     And the body than raiment?

     Behold the fowls of the air:
         for they sow not,
         neither do they reap,
         nor gather into barns;

     Yet your heavenly Father feedeth them.

     Are ye not much better than they?

     Which of you by taking thought
         can add one cubit unto his stature?
               —Matthew 6:25–27

If we are well satisfied with our civilization, our culture, our institutions, it would not be unreasonable to say that Jesus is our great enemy. He is the alien, the fleeting ghost moving in and out among the shadows of the private mind, and of the collective mind. A wanderer. Where can he find a place in which he can be at home? He challenges the very grounds of the common assumptions upon which we live, day after day. He was no radical political reformer; nor was he a radical social reformer. But he was a religious man who, out of his inner experience of God, spoke judgment upon the established order.

God was the source and the touchstone, the point of referral, for Jesus. We have heard this all our days and there is nothing new in it until we see the difference such a point of referral makes when applied in our lives. Jesus taught that God is the Father of Life, of all Mankind; that the character of the relationship by which men are bound one to another does not derive primarily from one man's feeling for another, but from a man's interpretation of the will of God for him in his relationship to another. To Jesus, each human being is of infinite worth to God and before God; there is One God, and to that One God every human being in the world is related. A man's significance is precisely in that fact. Therefore, in dealings with other human beings I must act from within that presupposition. How terrible that is! It means that the social classifications, within which my life and your life exist, have no validity. A Republican and a Democrat, a Socialist and a Communist, a Methodist and a Baptist, a Buddhist and a Hindu, a poor man and a rich man, a male human being and a female human being, an ignorant person and a learned person, a sick person and a well person—none of these classifications has meaning before God. Each one is a human being, not because of his social standing, not because of his relation to another human being, not according to his context, or to the character of his life—No! Every human being *as a human being* relates to God. That is the point! The chief concern, then, of each of us, according to this concept of Jesus, is his acceptance of this relation to God. However I feel toward another human being, whatever bearing my relationship with him may have on the fate of my family, or the fate of my class, or the fate of my nation, the question that I must ask is: What is the will of God for me?

Into the established pattern of life Jesus brings this radical principle; and chaos results. As this principle invades the structure of our familiar human relationships and our private lives, not peace but a sword emerges in our midst.

Turn and look at the pattern of life of the normal, ordinarily resourceful human being. As I look at my life, I see a wide variety of scattered loyalties, scattered and splintered devotions. Some basis of order, of integration, does govern my experience, but it is likely to be a secondary principle, rather than a primary one. A man's principle of integration, around which the details of his life move in constellations, may be his work, his vocation. Or it may be something less significant, his golf, his neurosis. Every human being has a series of little centers of integration in his life that express themselves perhaps in simple habits, simple etiquettes with reference to things that are of no basic or perhaps no ultimate consequence. Have you ever seen someone whose whole life became disorganized for the day because the breakfast coffee was cold? That's what I mean.

Instead of all this absorption with detail, Jesus insists upon an absolute loyalty to God. The questions which he raises about our pattern of life are these: "Do you dare yield the 'nerve center' of your consent to what you believe is the will of God, as your basic principle of integration, rather than to some secondary something, important as that is to you—vocation, family, business, anxiety, money, position, class, race? Do you dare shift the center of focus of your being away from these significant loyalties, that have defined the character of your living, and embrace what, deep within you, you know to be the ultimate devotion of your life?" Your life is the lung through which your loyalties breathe. If you are not willing to yield complete loyalty to the will of God, if you prefer to give first place to your secondary loyalties, you may try to establish a way of relating yourself to Jesus that will not disturb the pattern of your living. On the other hand, if you do accept Jesus' way for you then there is introduced at once into your life a principle that at first reduces to complete chaos the whole network of your relations. That is what Jesus says. Do you wonder that he can find no place to be at home in our whole world? Do you wonder?

# 3.  NOT PEACE—A SWORD—II

### MEDITATION

*O Lord, thou hast searched me, and known me.*

*Thou knowest my downsitting and mine uprising,*
*thou understandest my thought afar off.*

*Thou compassest my path and my lying down,*
*and art acquainted with all my ways.*

*For there is not a word in my tongue,*
*but, lo, O Lord, thou knowest it altogether.*

*Thou hast best me behind and before,*
*and laid thine hand upon me.*

*Such knowledge is too wonderful for me;*
*it is high, I cannot attain unto it.*

## CONCERNING PEACE

Whither shall I go from thy spirit?
  or whither shall I flee from thy presence?

If I ascend up into heaven,
  thou art there:

If I make my bed in hell,
  behold, thou art there.

If I take the wings of the morning,
  and dwell in the uttermost parts of the sea;

Even there shall thy hand lead me,
  and thy right hand shall hold me.

If I say, Surely the darkness shall cover me;
Even the night shall be light about me.

Yea, the darkness hideth not from thee;
  but the night shineth as the day:

The darkness and the light are both alike to thee.

For thou hast possessed my reins:
  thou hast covered me in my mother's womb.

I will praise thee;
  for I am fearfully and wonderfully made:
Marvellous are thy works;
  and that my soul knoweth right well.

My substance was not hid from thee,
  when I was made in secret,
  and curiously wrought in the lowest parts of the earth.

Thine eyes did see my substance,
  yet being unperfect;
And in thy book all my members were written,
  which in continuance were fashioned,
  when as yet there was none of them.

101

How precious also are thy thoughts unto me, O God!

How great is the sum of them!
If I should count them,
they are more in number than the sand:
When I awake,
I am still with thee.

Search me, O God,
and know my heart:
Try me,
and know my thoughts:

And see if there be any wicked way in me,
And lead me in the way everlasting.

—Psalm 139:1–18, 23–24

### READING

Between the idea
And the reality
Between the motion
And the act
Falls the shadow.

This quotation from T. S. Eliot's "The Hollow Men" puts into crisp words one of the oldest problems of the human spirit. There is always the riding frustration to all human effort that makes it fall short of the intent, the clear-cut purpose. Sometimes it is very difficult for the idea, the plan or ideal to be clearly defined. To know precisely what it is that we want to do is often a very torturous process. It is hard to make up one's mind about goals because motives are often mixed and confused.

And yet, the Great Frustration is not at the point of the elusive and indefinable goal, purpose, or end. It is rather at the point of determining how to span the gulf that lies between the goal and its fulfillment, the purpose and its realization. The gulf is deep and wide between the dream and the implementation. Look at any achievement of your life, however simple or elaborate! There is almost always one judgment that you can pass upon it—it is so much less than what you were sure you had in mind. As the dream lay nestled in your mind untouched by the things that sully or corrupt, you were stirred to the deep places within by its rightness, by its beauty, by its truth. Then the time of birth was upon you—the dream took its place among the stuff of your daily round. Looking upon it now, it is so much less than what it seemed to be before. It is ever thus.

A man sees the good and tries to achieve it in what he thinks, says, and does. With what results? You know your answer. How often have you felt—the good I see I do not. Or the good I see I achieve only in such limited, inadequate ways that I wonder even about the vision itself. Always there is the shadow—always there is the wide place between the dream and its fulfillment— the goal and its achievement. Therefore, only the stupid are arrogant because of achievements, however grand they may be. The achievement is a source of pride, perhaps, when compared with what other men have done—once in a great while, this is so! But when the achievement is compared with what was the high level of the intent, then the achievement itself is seen for what it is—a poor, weak manifestation of the dream. It is well that it is so. The dreams, the goals, the ideals keep the spirit harassed and the sand ever hot under the feet. There can be no rest for the spirit in anything less than the perfection which is God. This fact indicated somewhat the measure of the meaning of human life! It was no mere utterance of an anxious piety, *these words of the Master, "You, therefore, must be perfect, as your heavenly Father is perfect."*

---

Jesus approached all of life from within the tremendous vitality of his religious experience. The incentive in his mind was always spiritual and religious. Therefore, his attack upon the problems of human existence and human destiny was primarily from within the meaning of religion and religious experience rather than from within the context of morality, of ethics, or of any kind of reform. He introduced into the behavior patterns of men what may be called, for lack of a better term, the *principle of concretion.*

Jesus' profound emphasis is on persons. Every man is directly related to God. The soul of every man belongs to God. The ultimate responsibility of every man is to God. Human relationships, those of one man to another, provide the climate, the atmosphere, the condition, in which the individual, by dealing justly and kindly with his fellows, may seek to define for himself the meaning of the Will of God. This sounds very simple. But when we introduce this emphasis into our private life or into the social context in which we live, we introduce a principle of divisiveness, a principle of disorder, a principle of disturbance. This is true because people tend to live in relation to one another on the *principle of abstraction* rather than on the principle of concretion. Wherever the principle of abstraction comes into contact with the principle of concretion, there is a clash, a terrible clash. This is the sword which Jesus said he had come to bring.

As a human being, I am always insisting that *I* be regarded according to the principle of concretion; but, I tend to relate to you in terms of a principle of abstraction. For instance, you say,

"This man is my husband!" That is an abstraction. To it belongs a whole etiquette, a whole behavior pattern, a whole set of associations, by which his "husbandness" is defined. All the time, however, he feels himself to be concrete. Or, here is a child. For instance, I have a daughter. My temptation all the time is to deal with her on the basis of the principle of abstraction. I say, "This is my daughter!" All sorts of things belong to that cluster of ideas that surround the daughter notion. But, all the time, my daughter is insisting that only incidentally is she a "daughter." She has her own hopes, fears, dreams. To herself, she is concrete. She is always trying to break the category of abstraction by insisting that she be regarded as a person. Now, the moment I begin regarding her on the basis of the principle of concretion, I must instantly revise the notion that I have built up on the basis of the principle of abstraction. What does this involve?

When a child tries to talk to father or mother on the basis of the principle of concretion, he often finds he is dealing with a person who is virtually a stranger to him. Unless father and child, or mother and child, have been able to work out the kind of relationship between them in which there is real understanding, the child turns his back upon all the wisdom, knowledge, experience, a parent may have, and seeks to get these same resources in another situation in which the principle of concretion is operating.

When we apply the distinction between the abstract and the concrete to a wider context of relationships, we see some very interesting things. We see what a sword is introduced when we look at national ideas. We constantly deal with other nations on the basis of the principle of abstraction. This is a German. This is a Russian. This is a Scandinavian. But all the time, the Russian, from within his own context, is a man with hopes, dreams, ambitions, weaknesses, strengths—in short, a human being. When we consider group relations, we come upon the same principle. Much of the turmoil we are having now in the southern part of the United States centers in this area of confusion. These men, Negro and white, are dealing with each other in terms of the principle of abstraction. Even the law defines each of the two groups in terms of abstraction.

I knew of a case in which a Negro lodge official was told he must have his books balanced by a white man because "no Negro can possibly be a certified public accountant in the state of Georgia." At that time there was a Negro who was a C.P.A. in the state of Georgia. He lived in a city many miles removed from the home of the lodge official. How could he prove his identity and his credentials *in absentia?* This is what happened. The accountant copied the definition of a Negro as set forth in the state statute of Georgia. This was an abstraction. Then he took this before a notary and attested to the fact that it applied to him—the operation of the principle of concretion. When this was accomplished, he was able to get the business.

Let me illustrate the clash I am talking about out of my own experience. When I was a boy living in Florida, one of my after-school jobs was raking leaves in a certain large yard. The leaves fell with a great deal of insistence. One day, as I was at work on this job, the daughter in the family, a little white girl about five years old, decided to follow me around. She had great fun picking up pretty leaves for me to see; and she became a nuisance to me because she scattered the leaves as fast as I would rake them into a pile. Then I would have to do all my work over again. Finally, I said, "Why don't you go in the house? If you don't stop bothering me, I will tell your mother and she will call you in." The child became incensed, rushed up to me, pulled a pin out of her pinafore, and stuck me with it. And when I reacted

naturally, she said, "But that didn't hurt you, you can't feel."
The principle of abstraction. As soon as it challenges the principle of concretion, the sword is introduced.

When Gandhi insisted that the untouchables of India be called "Children of God," the principle of concretion moved in to challenge the principle of abstraction. Wherever it moves, the sword is introduced. Many of the behavior patterns by which we all live tend to be worked out on the basis of the kind of integration that arises from abstractions. The moment we are required, as a result of something new in the context of our living, to embrace the principle of concretion, a new behavior pattern restructures our whole climate.

There is another way in which this operates. In our religious observances even Jesus is, again and again, pushed into a category that is defined by the principle of abstraction. So long as he is held there, we absolve ourselves of the necessity for the introduction of the principle of concretion, though it was on this basis that he lived, worked, dreamed, suffered, died. In the name of religion, abstractions may march in good standing along with the most anti-Christian, anti-decent behavior. Certain organizations—councils they are called—that are being formed in the south insist that the members must believe in Jesus Christ. That this requirement was also made by the old Ku Klux Klan is common knowledge. They safely embalm Jesus in a principle of abstraction and so protect themselves from having to deal with what he insisted upon—the principle of concretion. He said that the line from the individual human spirit to God is a direct line. The ultimate responsibility of the human spirit is not to any category of abstraction, but is intensely and utterly concrete. God holds the man responsible. Not the preacher! Not the parent! Not the politician! Not the American, nor the Russian, nor the Catholic, nor the Jew, nor the Protestant, nor the Hindu, nor the Atheist, nor the Free-Wheeler—God holds the man responsible! This is terribly concrete! I am responsible to God, I, the person! I have a name. I breathe. I eat. I sleep. I work. I am responsible! I can't hide behind any principle of abstraction. God seeks me out; whatever be the hiding place in which I try to guard my dignity. He does not get off my scent. Relentlessly, he tracks me down until at last, I, Howard Thurman, must answer to Him. If you recognize and acknowledge your responsibility to God, says Jesus, you may be persecuted, but you must not feel deserted by God. Rejoice and know that the sanction of God for your life is the only one that is valid. Believing that, wherever you move, in whatever you do, there the kingdom of God is at hand. Your very presence may introduce tension—the sword! But rejoice. Rejoice!

———◆———

*Forgive us, our Father, for blindness, for pride and arrogance of mind, for the subtle conceit that undermines the integrity of all that we think and feel and do. Accept us, O God, as we are, and leave us not alone as we separate one from the other, but bless our days and our coming together again.*

# PART V
## CONCERNING FESTIVALS

———— ❧ ————

## 1. THE ETERNAL LIGHT

### MEDITATION

A candle is a small thing.

But one candle can light another.

And as it gives its flame to the other,
see how its own light . . . increases!

YOU ARE SUCH A LIGHT.

Light is the power to dispel darkness.

You have this power to move back the darkness in yourself
and in others—with the birth of light created when one mind
illuminates another, when one heart kindles another, when one
man strengthens another.

And its flame also enlarges within you as you pass it on.

THROUGHOUT HISTORY children of darkness have tried to smother this passage of light from man to man. Throughout history dictators, large and small, have tried to darken, diminish and separate men by force.

But always in the end they fail.

For always somewhere in the world the light remains; ready to burn its brightest where it is dark; a light that began when God created the world:

". . . Who coverest Thyself with light as with a garment. . . ."

And every free people has remained free by resisting those who would extinguish in men the light of freedom, of love, of truth.

TO DO OUR DAILY PART to increase this light, we must remember that a candle alone is a small thing, a man alone is a small thing, a nation alone is a small thing.

Remembering this, we must recognize something much more than our indispensability to others. We must also remember their indispensability to us. . . .

"THESE LIGHTS WE NOW KINDLE . . ."

These words accompany the lighting of Hanukkah candles in the home, and in the heart, to commemorate the eternal bridge of light which reaches from Creation itself to the radiant spirit of free men.

In this spirit is celebrated the Festival of Hanukkah—the Festival of Light—wherein the candle that gives its light to the others is called "the servant candle."

You, too, are strongest . . . when you serve.

—Hanukkah, 1955, message of The Jewish Theological
Seminary of America

In one of Petrarch's *Letters of Old Age* appear these words:

When a word must be spoken to further a good cause, and those whom it behooves to speak remain silent, anybody ought to raise his voice, and break a silence which may be fraught with evil. . . . Many a time a few simple words have helped further the welfare of the nation, no matter who uttered them; the voice itself displaying its latent powers, sufficed to move the hearts of men.

It is so easy to underrate the potential power of one word spoken at the critical moment. We say to ourselves sometimes that because we are not famous or learned or rich or powerful or gifted, our word means nothing in the presence of a great injustice. Who would pay attention to us? Many good causes are hindered, often nameless persons are brought to an untimely end, because "those whom it behooves to speak remain silent"; and because they do not speak, we do not speak. It is important to remember that there is no limit to the power of any single voice when it is the only outlet, the only channel, for justice or righteousness in a given situation. The silence of the high and mighty sometimes gives greater power to the simple voice of a solitary individual. During practically any week, you may be faced with some great wrong or some simple but gross expression of injustice and there is no one to speak but you. Do not be silent; there is no limit to the power that may be released through you.

———◆———

There is a strange and awe-inspiring aura around the fateful movement of the Jewish community down through the centuries, something that is difficult to understand, something that perhaps cannot be quite understood. Here is at work what seems to be not a human genius but a spiritual genius as the motive power of the aspiration and the activity and the influence of a people. Where would our Western culture and tradition be today if there were removed from the quality of our thinking and feeling the witness of the prophets of Israel?

In the year 165 B.C. the temple at Jerusalem was recaptured from the Syrians by Judas Maccabaeus. It was cleansed and purified in accordance with the tradition of his faith. One bottle of pure oil was found to kindle the light on the altar, just enough for one day. The tradition is that this light burned in a miraculous manner for eight days. It is perhaps only incidental, though it seems significant, that this took place at the winter solstice. The burning of the lights is a tradition as old as human striving and aspiration. How often a light has become involved in the ceremony and the expression of the collective devotion of a people! The lighting of the light! Its single claim to distinction is that as long as it burns, darkness can't put it out. It must have been a very terrifying thing for early man to watch the days get shorter and shorter and shorter, until at last one day was so short that it almost didn't start. There must have been those who said, "Perhaps there is something we can do to stay the darkness. Even though the lights in the heavens seem to be going out, we believe in light and perhaps, if we can *light* a light, our little light can hold the darkness back until the big light can catch its breath and roll the darkness back." Thus lights burn at Christmastime; lights burn at the Jewish festival of lights, Hanukkah.

It may be well to recall a little of the history that led to the lighting of this particular lamp in Jerusalem. On the Syrian throne was Antiochus IV, who said that he was a God, and adopted as his second name Epiphanes because that meant "God manifest." One day out of each month, the anniversary date of his birth, he set aside for the people to worship him. At the center of the temple in Jerusalem he had erected both an altar to Jupiter and an image of himself. Similar altars had also been placed all over Palestine and Antiochus ordered that the Torah should be torn up and destroyed; circumcision was forbidden; and one was required to eat the flesh of the hog. When one man sainted in Israel, Eleazar, refused to contaminate his body and his spirit by tasting the flesh of swine, he was slowly tortured to death. Any women who were discovered taking their sons to be circumcised were lifted bodily and thrown from the city wall, that their skulls might be smashed on the rocks beneath. Such a ruler was Antiochus Epiphanes, nicknamed even by his friends Antiochus Epimanes, which means half-mad.

The representatives of this madman went to the villages and towns of Palestine and in each ordered the people to assemble and to worship this king, this heathen god. In the little village of Modin was a man called Mattathias who, with his five sons, lived on the road between Joppa and Jerusalem. He was not an aristocrat but belonged to the descendants of the priests. When ordered to bow before the image of Antiochus, he refused, and lest the whole community be destroyed in reprisal for the mad act of this Mattathias, one young man rose up from the group to make the sacrificial offering. As he was about to do so in defiance of the law and the judgment of Israel, Mattathias slew him with his own hands. Then with his sons he fled to the hills where he made guerrilla war upon Antiochus. He died soon after and leadership fell to his son Judah. For many years this band of guerrillas, enlarged by some others who had rallied around the banner of Israel, laid siege to the citadel at Jerusalem. The forces of Antiochus finally barricaded themselves at the temple and there they were destroyed utterly. But when the temple deliverers sought to light the light upon the altar, they found only enough oil for one day. Yet it burned miraculously for eight days. The light has not gone out since. It is the eternal light seen in every Jewish synagogue.

I think that it is not an exaggeration to say that the re-establishing of the worship of the One God of Israel, at this critical crossroads in human history, saved for all subsequent generations the One God "ethically-concerned," worship out of which came both Christianity and Mohammedanism. Israel had conceived of God as moral will. This moral will expressed itself in a series of mighty events: the creation of existence and the creation of life. It was also manifested in a covenanted community, that was related to Him in terms of obedience to His will and was responsive to His concerns. It is interesting that this aspect of the unique covenanted community, which we see arising out of the encounter of the heart of Israel with its God, moves full-orbed into Christianity. What was the covenanted community of Israel becomes the covenanted community of Christian believers—the Church. A single movement, a single process of the One God. He is moral and ethical will. To worship God and God alone is the be-all and end-all of man's life and purpose. To worship anything less is not only idolatry but blasphemy. Every dictator has said, "I am the state; and the devotion of all the people must be rallied around me"; governments too have claimed central place in the devotion and the worship of their people. Every one of them has been wrecked by this fundamental and basic insistence that inspired the life of Mattathias and Judah and a long line of men and women through the years since. As Mattathias knew, there is One God and One God only. He is moral and ethical will!

Now a second thing is important here. It is easy to take refuge, in the presence of evil, within the limitations of one's own little life. It is easy to say, "Nobody will pay any attention to me"; "I don't count"; "I'm not eloquent"; "I don't have any money"; "I am not in a strategic position"; "I am ignorant"—to make all sorts of excuses for taking no action. But when I feel that a thing is wrong, if I am silent, then it may be that the evil thing continues or that the right thing goes unfilled. Mattathias acted. We don't know what iknd of energy is floating around us by which, if we dare tap it, we ourselves, little and insignificant as we are, may be energized. The simplest instrument may become the channel through which the eternal power and redemptive spirit of God can spill over human need, redeeming it, salvaging it, making it whole.

A story was told to me once about a mother who became increasingly disturbed because her little boys, instead of eating their breakfast, wanted to play with the cut-out soldiers that were taken from their cereal box. Each boy had his own army and their mother found that their competition and struggle spilled out in a lot of other ways during the day. She talked with their teachers about it and learned that some other parents had been complaining about the same thing. She talked with her minister; he said it was a bad kind of education. But neither teacher nor minister had any cure. Then she decided she would do *something* because nobody else seemed ready to do *anything*. She wrote a letter to the manufacturers of the cereal, describing what was happening to her little boys and to her neighbors' little boys. In course of time, she got a reply saying that her letter had been shown to a psychologist, to an educator, and to a clergyman. All three agreed that she was right. As of the day of the receipt of her letter, all boxes with guns and soldiers on them were called in and animal figures were substituted. The individual cannot sense what may be in the brooding mind of God, seeking for some access to the lives of His children. It is thee the Angel may be calling, if you will hear.

There is one final thing to be said in this matter. Mattathias held his life cheap in comparison with the accomplishing of what he knew he must do. It is entirely possible for a man to place upon his physical life such extreme value that he will never know what it means to be a free spirit. If you place upon your physical life an ultimate value, then in order to save your own life you will be ready to betray yourself, your friends, your God, your family, just that you be permitted to live. Alternatively, when a man takes a stand for something that is more important in his sight than whether he lives or dies—in the moment of his self-relinquishment he may be free for the first time in his life.

For what are you willing, for what am I willing, to give up life? Is there anything in your experience that has come to defy all other meaning, so that on behalf of it you will gladly yield your life? If you live having betrayed this commitment, it were better that you had never been born. To live with the freedom of God in the heart means to recognize the principle that perhaps the only way by which you may save your life is to lose it. This is the word of Hanukkah. And it is the word of Christmas. "Whosoever will lose his life for my sake shall find it." Perhaps when Jesus said those words the ghosts of Mattathias and Judah were stalking across his horizon.

——————◆——————

*Walk beside us, O God, our Father, in the way that we take.*

# 2. THE FULLNESS OF TIME

### MEDITATION

*Christmas is a mood, a quality, a symbol. It is never merely a fact. As a fact it is a date on the calendar—to the believer it is the anniversary of an event in human history. An individual may relate himself meaningfully to the fact or the event, but that would not be Christmas.*

*The mood of Christmas—what is it? It is a quickening of the presence of other human beings into whose lives a precious part of one's own has been released. It is a memory of other days when into one's path an angel appeared spreading a halo over an ordinary moment or a commonplace event. It is an iridescence of sheer delight that bathed one's whole being with something more wonderful than words can ever tell. Of such is the mood of Christmas.*

The quality of Christmas—what is it? It is the fullness with which fruit ripens, blossoms unfold into flowers, and live coals glow in the darkness. It is the richness of vibrant colors—the calm purple of grapes, the exciting redness of tomatoes, the shimmering light on the noiseless stirring of a lake or sunset. It is the sense of plateau with a large rock behind which one may take temporary respite from winds that chill. Of such is the quality of Christmas.

The symbol of Christmas—what is it? It is the rainbow arched over the roof of the sky when the clouds are heavy with foreboding. It is the cry of life in the new-born babe when, forced from its mother's nest, it claims its right to live. It is the brooding Presence of the Eternal Spirit making crooked paths straight, rough places smooth, tired hearts refreshed, dead hopes stir with newness of life. It is the promise of tomorrow at the close of every day, the movement of life in defiance of death, and the assurance that love is sturdier than hate, that right is more confident than wrong, that good is more permanent than evil.

## READING

There must be always remaining in every man's life some place for the singing of angels, some place for that which in itself is breathlessly beautiful, and, by an inherent prerogative, throws all the rest of life into a new and creative relatedness, something that gathers up in itself all the freshets of experience from drab and commomplace areas of living and glows in one bright white light of penetrating beauty and meaning—then passes. The commonplace is shot through with new glory; old burdens become lighter; deep and ancient wounds lose much of their old, old hurting. A crown is placed over our heads that for the *rest of our lives we are trying to grow tall enough to wear. Despite all the crassness of life, despite all the hardness of life, despite all the harsh discords of life, life is saved by the singing of angels.*

———◆———

When I was a high school boy, one of my most impressive lessons was one in ancient history. In my textbook the chapter title was "The Fullness of Time." The author said that Jesus was born at a time when the world was at peace; that tranquillity and calmness were everywhere, thus creating a waiting moment. It is an interesting thought.

The fullness of time. Life seems to operate always in two dimensions, or at two levels. There are wide and comprehensive and vast purposes and, in them all, the little expressions of life are caught up, transformed, and given meaning. Dr. Brightman in his studies of the history of philosophy of religion lists the important, crucial, ethical, and religious movements in human history. He makes the very interesting observation that within the period between the eighth and fourth centuries B.C. most of these important philosophic, ethical, and religious movements began marching. Within that time span came the prophets of Israel, for instance; all of Greek philosophy; Zoroaster; all of the basic insights upon which modern life moves and which have structured the very grounds of modern life. It seems as if life were aware that it is necessary for the human race to have accumulated a backlog of distilled wisdom, of concentrated ethical and religious insight, with which, over a long time interval and at varying levels of awareness, it could be associated. This must have been absorbed against the day when there would be no time to tarry and think deeply over the central concerns of mind and spirit. Suppose the scientific revolution had preceded the exposure of the human race to sustained religious and philosophic insight. Suppose that all we know now about modern science as a tool, as a facility, as a discipline, had come before the human race had been aged a little in the ethical and religious and spiritual wood, as it were. Suppose that man had already mastered nature as he has since and had already reduced our whole planet to a little neighborhood. Do you see what is involved? As it is we have great anxiety as to whether or not we may destroy ourselves with these tremendous weapons. All the mastery that we have gathered over nature, the implements of destruction that we have created—we are concerned about these, lest with them we destroy our civilization. How much more vast would be our plight if in the background of human thought and human living there were not the wisdom of the prophets, if there were not the philosophic and ethical insight of the Greeks, if there were no life of Jesus! Suppose all of that were in the future, how great and how tragic would be our fate at this moment! But No! Life seems to have moved on the basis of this concept of the fullness of time.

Consider another step. Suppose we had had this whole education in modern science and the world of nature, suppose we had behind us the shrinking of the world and the making of it all into one little neighborhood, without there having been anywhere on this planet the peculiar learning experience which is the unique genius of America. Think about it! Here as a result of processes that we do not quite understand, a few hundred years ago, from the ends of the earth there came to this region, between the two oceans, a multitude of people of different hues, of different cultures, of different language heritages, even of different faiths. For a long time these people were isolated between the Atlantic and Pacific Oceans, with a climate that was well-nigh ideal, with natural resources that made life almost self-contained. At the same time there brooded over this cross section of human beings, creative, ethical, and political ideals, distilled from the movement of the spirit of God in generations of men of different kinds—ideals formulated in a political constitution and a bill of rights, and in conception of personality and of religion derived from the holy book. These political and spiritual and ethical ideals have tutored the American spirit despite all our blunders. Here we are, differing in so many ways that in any gathering of people anywhere in America, we are likely to come upon someone who speaks a language that the rest of us do not understand. During two hundred years under the relentless judgment of this kind of idealism, the results have crept into law, crept into custom, and crept into social attitudes. It is as if life had anticipated a moment when all kinds of people, whose traditions and customs vary widely, would be thrown together in one neighborhood because of man's mastery over nature. Now suppose this had taken place before anywhere on this planet was there any laboratory, any schooling experience, taming some of the wildness and self-assertedness out of the spirit of man, readying him in all sorts of little ways for getting along with people of different background, culture, and color. Suppose all of this—and imagine how desperate would be our situation. Instead what happened? Between these two oceans several millions of people of many varieties have been learning how to live together, as if the whole world were like that; and suddenly the whole world *is* like that. In the fullness of time a new day is upon us!

Besides this historical application of the idea of the fullness of time there is a second dimension. It applies to the ways in which an individual sees himself—what he dreams, what he sees, what he feels, what he does—as the fruition of some vast, great, creative, and redemptive purpose. Jesus so conceived of himself when he visited the synagogue after the temptation in the wilderness. The leader of the congregation, as was the custom, offered Jesus the scroll from which to read the morning lesson. Jesus opened the scroll; and this is what he read: "The Spirit of the Lord is upon me, because he has anointed me to preach the good news to the poor. He has sent me to proclaim release to the captives and recovering of sight to the blind, to set at liberty those who are oppressed." Then, as he closed the book, he said: "These words are now fulfilled in your hearing." In other words he said, "I am the fulfillment of these words, because they speak directly to my own mind and my own spirit, and in them I see what I am to be and to do." How do you relate to the fullness of time—you? Is there anything in your life, any movement, any current, that makes you feel as if great meanings, purposes, and processes are being fulfilled at the level of your living? Or are you merely living within the limitations of the little events by which your daily life is defined?

As we look at the life of Jesus, we discover that there was no great dazzling character to his daily living experience. He loved children. They responded to him. He talked with the woman at the well. He ate, kept company with the commonplace people. When we sum up his life, the most important thing that can be said about his life is nothing that he did, but something that he was. He did a thousand little things, but all of them were infused with the profoundest awareness of his life as a living instrument in the hands of God. He was available to the living God *totally*, so that in what he did and in what he said there was always the touch of the spirit and the life of God. We can make ourselves available to the fullness of time by learning how to be unanimous within ourselves and to make of that unanimity a living offering to God at the level of our own personal, private insight. When we do that, then the fullness of time is born in us, and the vast purposes of God become flesh and blood in us. No greater wish could I make for each of us than that we become the complete expression of the will of God at the level where we live and work and play and function. To the degree to which we do that, His purposes are fulfilled in us. This is to know what it means to be a child of God.

———◆———

*Give unto our spirits the strength that we need to think Thy thoughts after Thee and to be in all of the little ways, our Father, Thy children. Dismiss us with Thy Spirit; leave us not alone in the way that we take.*

# 3. A NEW HEAVEN AND A NEW EARTH
## (AS WE FACE A NEW YEAR)

*Bit by bit, we put aside the pretensions of our days as we sit together in quietness in the presence of God. It is strange how as we sit in His presence so many things that yesterday seemed important, even crucial, have somehow lost their significance. The ambitions by which our waking hours are harassed and our nights tortured in dreams, do not now seem very important. The injuries which we nourished all during the year that is past, injuries inflicted upon us by those who walked the way with us or who blundered into our path, injuries that seemed so unforgiveable—strange, but they don't seem to matter as we sit here in the quietness of His presence.*

*It is a good thing to be here, to sit together, to feel flowing*

124

from one another the same deep anxiety of spirit for purity of mind and heart and body, for renewal of spirit that the hard tasks may be taken up afresh, and to know that we are not alone, that we have one another and the great host of seekers all over the world. What is more important, as we sit here, we know that we have Him.

Thus, our Father, who loves us into repentance of our sins, who loves our cowardice into courage, who loves our hopelessness into faith, O God, Thy love overwhelms us, O God, God, our Father!

### READING

"Be still and know that I am God!"

Deep and prophetic, this watching hour!

After the struggle, the stillness. After the clamor to achieve, the hearkening that receives. Is this that surrender men have spoken of as the way to life, that yielding?

Awful is Thy silence brooding over chaos, surely the very gestation of the spirit! Creation waiteth for the manifestation of the sons of God. Ay, the sons, of the spirit born, else never born.

"Canst thou by searching find out God?"

How I believed I might throw my nets about Thee, and if not, it would only be because, forsooth, there was no Thee to capture! Oh, rebuke me not for this presumptuous sin! Behold, now I let Thee do Thy work, no way have I but this. In quietness and in confidence my strength shall be, and perhaps, my vision.

Does the coast take possession of the tide? Does the earth

reach out and dress itself with the sun? My soul waiteth for the Lord, yea, more than watchmen wait for the morning, more, more!

"And God said, 'Let there be light!' . . . And there was morning."

O God, I saw Thee push the black bolts back today and set ajar the Gates of Dawn, and the Spirit of Morning coming through at once was everywhere. The golden torrent of her hair she shook wide and free and lightly tiptoed up the sky, while all her trailing skirts spread glory; she blew a whisper through the woodland and it broke in song; she glanced along the streams and they mirrored heaven; she ran across the lawns, through gardens enamel petalled and aroma drunk. They stood unutterably still and rich, as if their soul had come.

Glorious God, I saw Thy Morning,
and it seemed like resurrection to a life once
dead in trespasses and sins.

—OSWALD W. S. McCALL

———◆———

"Behold," says the prophet and seer in that rather fabulous and puzzling book of Revelation, "I saw a new heaven and a new earth." Very daring words they are and it is important for us to recognize that these words came out of a background of struggle and pain and tragedy and persecution. They testify to the fact that there is something about the human spirit that is able to project itself out of any dilemma which may be facing it, and to act as if the dilemma had been resolved.

Sometimes, however, we are imprisoned by our dilemmas. I remember once I had to go to the hospital with an attack of tonsillitis. I amused myself during the two days I was there by trying to remember how I felt when I did not have tonsillitis. I could hardly do it. The tonsillitis had imprisoned me. My ceiling was zero. But only temporarily. Then I escaped the clutches of my present fact and knew that life would go on again as if this illness had never been.

It is this quality in the human spirit upon which rides always the apocalyptic hope. There is profound insight here. It is to this that I call your attention as we face a new year. And what is this insight? There is no experience, there is no event, there is no manifestation of life, there is no interpretation of the meaning of life, there is no dogma concerning the significance of life, that can possibly exhaust all that life has to say. Yet, we are to deal with truth as we see it, as if it is all the truth there is, as if it embraced all the possibilities. When we act upon that assumption, we know, at the same time, that ahead of us is far more than we now think, far more than we now believe, and that our present truth may even in time become error.

Let us think this through. Here are very profound implications for our lives. For we must know that we are not through growing, developing; that man is not finished; that perhaps the world is not finished; but that also there is inherent in life itself that which places limitations upon us.

Suppose a tree couldn't stop growing; suppose your feet couldn't stop growing. But just grew on and on and there were nothing you could do about it. It is like a figure in Zarathustra called the "cripple in reverse," the man who had the ear lobe that extended from his head down to the ground—an ear lobe growing and growing, which apparently couldn't stop. It is a wonderful thing that inherent in the life process are limitations, so that though new things start growing, old things also stop growing.

I am always reminded that the experience which may be mine

at a particular moment may be an experience in which things are stopping. Or it may be an experience in which things are just beginning. It is important that I know which process is taking place. An intimate part of growing into life is the development of a sensitiveness, an apprehension of process in its totality, that I may be enabled to know the character of the event with which I am dealing. Then I will not act in the house of death unnaturally by not accepting it; nor will I act in the house of life unnaturally by not accepting it. All of this is to say that there is inherent in life and brooding over the life of man the creative mind and spirit of the living God. This concept may express itself in the mind of the prophet or in the sensitiveness of the religious spirit. Then the individual deals with the elements in his world as if they were, as indeed they are, doors that open into unexplored areas and unknown territories. When the writer of Revelation dreams, he says that he sees a new heaven and a new earth. If heaven is where God dwells, and there is a new heaven, what does that mean? Is the seer saying that God moves out more and more in creative exploration, that before there can be a new earth there must be a new heaven? When we dream, we tend to reverse the process. We talk about, and we work for, a new earth while we try to keep an old heaven. And we can't do it.

A new earth—we talk about it! One world—we talk about it! We try to get sufficient dynamic, sufficient conception, sufficient insight, from an old heaven, an old dogma, an old theological discipline, to provide power, insight, guidance, strength, substance, for a new world. And we can't do it.

But a new heaven! The dream of a new heaven, with all that that implies, works over the stubborn and often unyielding stuff of the old earth until at last out of the very heartthrob of the new heaven is born the new earth.

## CONCERNING FESTIVALS

There can be no greater hope, no greater stirring of the mind and the spirit, as we face the new year with all of its withering disillusions and its grounded despair, than that we be visited by the glory of a new heaven. Wherever we are, however we are functioning, whatever responsibilities are ours—if we capture the mood, the spirit, the intensity of a new heaven to steady us and to strengthen us, we shall walk through the "crud" of the old earth in preparation for a new earth—a new earth which will be the heritage of little babies and little puppies and little kittens yet to come. What a wonderful thing to make that kind of demand upon today and tomorrow!

Behold, there shall be a new heaven and a new earth, because the new heaven is already born in the heart and the spirit and the life of any man anywhere who has made the great and central surrender to God. Yes, this is it!

# 4. THE QUEST FOR IMMORTALITY

## MEDITATION

*"The only strength for me is to be found in the sense of a personal presence everywhere, it scarcely matters whether it be called human or divine; a presence which only makes itself felt at first in this and that particular form and picture. . . . Into this presence we come, not by leaving behind what are usually called earthly things; or by loving them less, but by living more intensely in them, and loving more what is really lovable in them; for it is literally true that this world is everything to us, if only we choose to make it so, if only we 'live in the present' because it is eternity."* Thus wrote Richard Nettleship in a letter in 1897.

In a very real sense we are earthbound creatures, caught always in the rigid context by which our experiences are defined.

The particular fact or experience which we are facing at the moment, or the memory of other particular facts or experiences from other moments, these are our openings, these are the doors through which we enter into wider meanings, into wider contexts. When our little world of particular experiences seems to be illumined by more, much more than itself, and we seem to be caught up into something bigger than our little lives, we give to such moments special names. They become watershed times. We mark the times in special ways, with special symbols. If it is the love of man and woman, it is the ring, the ceremonial or the deep stillness of intimate disclosure; if it is the chance or deliberate encounter with the spirit of God at the peak of joy, the emptying of the soul in suffering, or the fragmented activities of the daily round, there is the sense of Altar, the searching phrase from the holy book, or the gathered tear and the quickening pulse beat. At such times and myriad others perhaps, we know that we live our way deeply in the present only to discover that we are invaded by the Eternal.

Sensitize our spirits, our Father, that we may tread reverently in the common way, mindful that the glory of the Eternal is our companion. May we shrink not from the present intensity of our experiences lest we turn away from the redeeming power of Thy Perfect Love.

### READING

Often there seems to be a clearly defined limit to human endurance. Each one of us has had the experience of what seems to us to be exhaustion. At such a time we seem to be taking the last possible step, to be up against a demand to which we can give no more in an effort to meet it. In simple ways we experience this. You are very weary, "exhausted" is the quick word used. In addition you are sleepy. If you cannot get to bed you are sure that you will go to sleep even in an upright, standing position. Then something happens. It may be a friend comes by to see you, a friend whose path has not crossed yours in several years. It may be that there are tidings of good news or tragedy. At any rate, something happens in you—the result, you are awake, recovered or even excited. A few minutes before the weariness had closed in like a dense fog.

Of course, our knowledge about our bodies and our minds gives to us an increasingly satisfying explanation of this kind of experience. The important thing, however, is the fact that beyond our zero point of endurance there are vast possibilities. The precise limitations under which we live our particular lives cannot be determined. Usually the stimulus, the incentive, must come from the outside—be brought to us on the wings of external circumstance. This means that the power available to us in great demand is not ours to command. I wonder!

The simple fact of enduring human experience which is described above opens up a great vista for living. It cannot be that what is possible to our bodies and our nervous system by way of tapping the additional resource on demand is denied our spirits. The spirit in man is not easily vanquished. It is fragile and tough. You may fail again and again and yet something will not let you give up. Something keeps you from accepting "No" as a final answer. It is this quality that makes for survival of values when the circumstances of one's life are most against decency, goodness, and right. Men tend to hold on when there seems to be no point in holding on because they find that they must. Often it is at such a point that the spirit in man and the spirit of God blend into one creative *illumination. This is the great miracle and even the body and nervous system know this!*

———◆———

Life is often thought of as a pilgrimage. In such a view man's life is a movement on an isthmus between two continents. The apostle Paul expresses it: "Ye are a colony of heaven." Jesus says that in his Father's house are many mansions which we shall inherit. In certain of the pre-Christian philosophers there is the notion that man's life antedates birth. Thus his days are haunted by the memory of what was before his journey. He moves always under the aegis of another world which is his homeland. Time then is one of the important factors in any consideration of the quest for immortality or the quest for life eternal.

We begin with the concept of man as a binder of space. He is always involved in events, in experience. Much of his life is spent in trying to identify himself with events, with things which seem to say to him that they are more permanent than he is because they are tangible, they can be seen and felt and touched. We measure often the meaning of our own lives in terms of the events that take place.

When I lived in the college town of Oberlin, one summer's day a Greyhound bus punctured a tire on the public square. It was an event for the bus to tarry for a long time. People came to look around. Two ladies got out of the bus for exercise. As they walked up and down the public square, one of them smoked a little cigar. That was something because, in those days, even men at Oberlin College were not permitted to smoke. After that, whenever someone wanted to date an event in the village, he remarked, "It was the fall before the lady

smoked the cigar on the public square . . . or the spring before
. . . or the winter after . . ."

We measure the meaning of life in terms of events, for we
are binders of space. It is for this reason that death seems to
loom so large in our considerations. Death is the rupturing of
a time-locked sequence. We struggle to give a time-transcend-
ent quality to the thing that is time-locked and time-bound.
We are binders of space. We want to see, feel, and touch a
thing if we are to say it is real. There is a fevered quality in
this space-bound characteristic because everything in space dis-
appears. We are besieged by the presence of the threat of
disintegration of all time-space manifestations: things, people,
events. This inspires our fears and distracts our mind from
something else. It is precisely the fact that things, events, co-
exist with something else in our experience that defines what
seems to be the true and authentic significance of this quest of
the human spirit for the eternal.

Man is not only a space-binder but he is also a time-binder.
Think of it in simple ways, for instance. You are sitting here
before me. Since I began talking, you have been into last week,
next week; you have been into this afternoon, you have looked
at your dinner, you have thought about what you are going to
do tonight. All the time you have been present here before me.
There is a quality of your personality that is not only involved
in this space-binding dimension but also in the time-binding
dimension. You are a binder of time. You stand outside of your
event, outside of your experience, outside of your fact.

It is this time-binding quality that seems to reveal the heart
of the meaning of all experience. No experience that we have
ever consumes all of us. Some part of us is always not quite in
the thing we are doing. There is a sense in which we are a
participant in our experience and at the same time an observer

of the experience. We are both observers and participants. There is no experience of our lives that is quite capable of rubbing out the line between man the observer and man the participant except in those moments when all of the boundaries of personality have been removed and we blend with something totally. For instance, a man sees a beautiful sunset. Sometimes, not always, in his encounter with the sunset he loses a sense of sunset-awareness and touches a quality of which the sunset was merely the opening, but with which the sunset is not identical. When that happens he the observer and he the participant become one; he becomes whole; he becomes, in that moment, something that includes time but has its significance out of time.

We may encounter this in other ways. When I was minister in residence of The Church for the Fellowship of All Peoples in San Francisco, I experienced this in a human relationship. For several weeks, every day, I visited a member of my church who was very ill. She had a disease for which there was no cure. For one-half hour every day, for several weeks, I read to her. Finally I stopped reading to her. I would simply go and sit. We would sit and "is" together. When I had to leave the city for several weeks, we entered into a very interesting little agreement. I worked out a timetable of the difference in the time between the Pacific coast and the various spots at which I would be stopping until I arrived in New York. At the same hour every morning, we met. For seven weeks every day with from two thousand to three thousand six hundred miles separating us, we touched each other outside of time.

This is to suggest that there is impinging always upon the experiences of man the space-binder, another quality, another dimension. It is the encounter with this other quality, this other dimension, that gives to time that which is eternal. I think that this quality toward which I am feebly feeling my way is God. Brooding over all of the events of life, over all the expressions of life, over all of the manifestations of life is the Mind and the Spirit of the Creator of life and wherever, with my little event, wherever, with my little experience, I am able to reach through it, I touch the Eternal. Something calls to me at a level in me that is deeper than the events of my life and the experiences of my days.

It is not an accident then, that approached from a thousand different angles the human spirit at last comes upon the same basic notion, that makes of the experience of love, for instance, the clue to the eternal. Now why? When I love I am always trying to get beyond the manifestation of the other—trying to get behind the features, behind the talents, behind the gifts, behind all the symbols of the personality. In order for the symbol to be sacramental, I must somehow touch that which is behind the façade, behind the manifestation, behind the expression, the thing that is outside the manifestation, but glorifies the manifestation. When I say, for instance, that some-one loves me, I am saying that I have been touched by some-thing at a depth in me that is beyond all of my limitations or qualities or virtues; beyond all that is good in me, beyond all that is evil in me. At last, in the awareness of that, I say, "Here is one who understands me." So, if it be true, as I think it is, that only in the love of God does man have that experience completely and fully, it is only here then that the meaning of the eternal takes on its binding character. So this is what the Master was talking about all the time. If you could get behind the tribulation, if you could get behind the time-space expression of disintegration that you call death, if you could get behind the life of one whom you call your enemy, God would be at once the answer to all that the heart yearns for and all

for which the spirit seeks. If you could trust God, you would
not be anxious, whether the circle that was broken would be
reunited or not, for you at last would be in communion with
Him from whom moves all things. To know God in this way
is Life eternal.

———◆———

*Give to the struggles of our mind and the halting inade-
quacies of our words the magic of Thy self, O God, our Father.
Dismiss us now from this place but walk beside us in the way
that we take reminding us that Thou hast made us for ourselves
and our souls are restless till they find their rest in Thee. O
Love of God, Love of God, Love of God.*

# PART VI

## CONCERNING CHRISTIAN CHARACTER

———————•◆•———————

# 1. THE LIGHT THAT IS DARKNESS

### MEDITATION

*How good it is to enter together into the fellowship of silent waiting, joined by one another's presence and by a great invisible host whose languages we cannot speak, whose knowledges we cannot grasp, but who, after the pattern of their own lives, their own needs, their own urgencies, are waiting somewhere in their own silence.*

*Each of us has the smell of life upon him, each of us has his problems, his needs—problems and needs which seem utterly personal and unique. Each of us has his joys—joys which seem utterly personal and unique. Each of us, in his own way, is trying to find answers to crucial questions. For some of us, the seeking has been long and hard, sometimes terrifying, sometimes heartbreaking. For some, the finding has frightened us* and given us an overbearing sense of responsibility and fear that dries up the springs of our activities and paralyzes our hopes. It is good to know that none is alone. It is good to feel the presence of others surrounding one's own privacy, spilling over into one's personal needs their strength and courage and hope.

To Thee, our Father, we expose the inward parts of our minds, holding back nothing, including in our offering the bad and the good, our failures and our successes, the things of which we are ashamed and the things in which we rejoice. Just as we are, without pretense, we expose to Thy light and Thy love, O God, our Friend and Redeemer.

### READING

"Let not thy will be set to sin." These searching words are from the book of Tobit. The attitude toward wrongdoing depends upon the character of the individual conscience. Conscience is rooted in the sense of value which is a part of the working equipment of personality. This sense of value is given; the content varies. Here the results of training, of observation, of social heritage, of religious experience and instruction, are made manifest. The judgment which says of a deed that it is wrong is always a reflection of the content of the individual's sense of value. So often such a judgment concerning wrongdoings does not involve the will of the individual. There seems to be an automatic, unreflective element in conscience. A man says: "I do not know why this is wrong, all that I know is, this is the way I feel about it." Or he may say: "I know my feeling of guilt for what I have done does not make sense, except to me."

Again and again we find ourselves reacting to the events and situations of our lives apart from our wills in the matter. It is the way we are trained, conditioned, taught. But this does not alter the fact of our responsibility for our acts and our reactions. An important part of living is the process by which the individual Will brings under its private jurisdiction the behavior of the individual. This is an essential element in any doctrine of self-mastery or, more accurately, of self-knowledge.

How many things have you done during the past week for which you have an after-the-event sense of responsibility, reflected in guilt, hostility, or pride—deeds which did not express your conscious intent because the doing of the deed did not come before your will for review: it was automatic, the result of long-established habits, training, conditioning? But once the deed was done and you were faced with the consequences, you realized that this kind of behavior was not your intent. The common cry is: I did not know. I did not understand.

It is important to make the full conquest of one's life pattern to the end the deeds of one's life will move more and more from the center of one's intent. Perhaps this is a goal that is never reached, but to work at it is to become increasingly mature and responsible. Meditation and prayer are helpful in providing a climate in which the deeds of one's life may be exposed and the character of the deeds understood. In such a climate, the most natural desire of the heart is the quiet utterance to God—

Let not my will be set to sin.

———◆———

An elderly lady nearing the end of her life paused to look back and recall some of its great moments. She wrote, among other things, about an occasion when she was walking in the country. She had been under great strain but suddenly the strain snapped like the breaking of a cord. To quote her own words: "I was flooded with an ineffable soul light which seemed to radiate from a great personality with whom I was in immediate touch. I felt it to be the touch of God. The ecstasy was beyond description. I was passing through a patch of beggar's grass with its wiry stems ending in feathery heads. Every head shone and glistened like pearls. I could hardly walk for the overwhelming sense of the Divine Presence and its joy. I almost saw God."

A little dog that had been walking quietly beside her looked up into her face at this point and began to bark in great excitement. I do not doubt that he saw in her face the great effulgence that she saw in the grass. I am glad to think that the glory of God is at the heart of beggar's grass as well as at the heart of men and that little dogs as well as human beings may see and rejoice.

The Fourth Gospel refers to the light that lighteth every man that cometh into the world. This light is the very ground of all being, the ground of creativity. Every creative thing has within it the signature of the Creator—His imprint, His stamp. You may think of the light in every man as that seal of the Creator. There no one is devoid of that light. Every man is born with it. We do not deserve any credit for having it. In truth we cannot get rid of it; it is an inherent part of our nature. There is something very consoling and refreshing about light in that sense, which perhaps in essence is metaphysical.

Jesus also refers to a light of another kind, light that is understanding, light that is meaning, light that is value. If that be darkness, then what a darkness it is! This is the light that we see in the dawning conscience and oh, how often we try to short-circuit that light. I have been watching the developing conscience in a puppy that has just come into our household. He has been told not to climb in a certain chair. It has been demonstrated to him that to do so is to find that the world is not friendly. So, when he gets up into this place that is forbidden, and I ask him to get down, he pretends that he does not hear me. He looks away from me. But because he remembers a time when we had an encounter about this matter, his eye steals slowly around to pick me up in his field of vision. He hears my voice and quickly swings his head back. He is trying to put his light out, but he cannot quite do it. Finally, with great reluctance, he jumps down from the chair.

Now that is the way we all behave, isn't it? We develop a certain knowledge, and the more skilled we become in the use of this knowledge, the greater becomes the strength of experience. But also, the more likely are we to disassociate ourselves from the responsibilities that are involved in having knowledge. This is the crucial peril of any kind of professionalism; for instance, I am a minister; again and again I am impressed with the fact that it is not easy to grow in sympathy and understanding of other people. It is very easy to become professionally a religious person, professionally a minister, and let my knowledge of the Bible, my knowledge of the history of the Church, my knowledge of the psychology of religion, become a substitute for getting on my knees, seeking forgiveness of my sins, wrestling with my spirit in the presence of God. If I let my knowledge become a substitute for my understanding, then the light that is in me becomes darkness. If the light that is in me becomes darkness, what a darkness.

Sometimes a man's light becomes darkness when he knows distinctly what he ought to do; he looks his duty, his responsibility, clearly in the face, calls every aspect of it by its right name, and then refuses to do it. When that happens, his light becomes darkness.

Just before he died, Hugh Price Hughes, celebrated Congregational minister of England, wrote an allegory which illustrates what I have in mind. He calls it "The City of Every-where."

"It is the tale of a man who might have been I, for I dreamed one time of journeying to that metropolis. I arrived early one morning. It was cold, there were flurries of snow on the ground and as I stepped from the train to the platform I noticed that the baggageman and the red cap were warmly attired in heavy coats and gloves, but oddly enough, they wore no shoes. My initial impulse was to ask the reason for this odd practice, but repressing it I passed into the station and inquired the way to the hotel. My curiosity, however, was immediately enhanced by the discovery that no one in the station wore any shoes. Boarding the streetcar, I saw that my fellow travelers were like-wise barefoot, and upon arriving at the hotel I found the bell-hop, the clerk and the habitues of the place were all devoid of shoes.

"Unable to restrain myself longer, I asked the ingratiating manager what the practice meant.

" 'What practice?' said he.

" 'Why,' I said, pointing to his bare feet, 'Why don't you wear any shoes in this town?'

" 'Ah,' said he, 'That is just it. Why don't we?'

" 'But what is the matter? Don't you believe in shoes?'

" 'Believe in shoes, my friend! I should say we do. That is the first article of our creed, shoes. They are indispensable to the well-being of humanity. Such chilblains, cuts, sores, suffer-ing, as shoes prevent! It is wonderful!'

" 'Well, then, why don't you wear them?' I asked, bewil-dered.

" 'Ah,' said he, 'That is just it. Why don't we?'

"Though considerably nonplused I checked in, secured my room and went directly to the coffeeshop and deliberately sat down by an amiable-looking gentleman who likewise conformed to the conventions of his fellow citizens. He wore no shoes. Friendly enough, he suggested after we had eaten that we look about the city. The first thing we noticed upon emerging from the hotel was a huge brick structure of impressive proportions. To this he pointed with pride.

" 'You see that?' said he. 'That is one of our outstanding shoe manufacturing establishments.'

" 'A what?' I asked in amazement. 'You mean you make shoes there?'

" 'Well, not exactly,' said he, a bit abashed, 'we talk about making shoes there and believe me, we have got one of the most brilliant young fellows you have ever heard. He talks most thrillingly and convincingly every week on this great subject of shoes. He has a most persuasive and appealing way. Just yesterday he moved the people profoundly with his exposition of the necessity of shoe-wearing. Many broke down and wept. It was really wonderful!'

" 'But why don't they wear them?' said I, insistently.

" 'Ah,' said he, putting his hand upon my arm and looking wistfully into my eyes, 'that is just it. Why don't we?'

"Just then, as we turned down a side street, I saw through a cellar window a cobbler actually making a pair of shoes. Excusing myself from my friend I burst into the little shop and asked the shoemaker how it happened that his shop was not overrun with customers. Said he, 'Nobody wants my shoes. They just talk about them.'

" 'Give me what pairs you have already,' said I eagerly, and paid him thrice the amount he modestly asked. Hurriedly, I returned to my friend and proffered them to him, saying 'Here, my friend, some one of these pairs will surely fit you. Take them, put them on. They will save you untold suffering.'

"But he looked embarrassed; in fact, he was well-nigh overcome with chagrin.

" 'Ah, thank you,' said he, politely, 'but you don't understand. It just isn't being done. The front families, well, I—'

" 'But why don't you wear them?' said I, dumbfounded.

" 'Ah,' said he, smiling with his accustomed ingratiating touch of practical wisdom, 'that is just it. Why don't we?'

"And coming out of the 'City of Everywhere' into the 'Here,' over and over and over that query rang in my ears: 'Why don't we? Why don't we? Why don't we?'—

"Why call ye me, 'Lord, Lord,' and do not the things I command you?"

If I know what I ought to do in a given situation, if I see the action that I should take in order to be true to the deepest thing in me, if I look it steadily in the eye and see not, the light that is in me becomes darkness. If the light becomes darkness, what a darkness!

And you putting out the light? Just think about it. In your own life this past week, did your light become darkness? Think about it without becoming morbid, depressed, or sentimental, but with a chastened spirit. Are you thinking right now about some decision that is waiting, about something that you know that you ought to do? And have you decided that you are not going to do it? When you made that decision, did the lights go out one by one and did you wonder what had happened to you? If the light that is in you be darkness, nothing outside of you can turn the light on again. Only you yourself can do that. Even God can't unless you give Him a hand.

———◆———

*Teach us, our Father, that if we nourish within ourselves those things that turn us away from the light, we shall spend*

our years stumbling through the darkness. *Teach us, our Father,
that if we be true to the light that is within us, we shall become
like Thee, and to become like Thee is the be-all and end-all of
our desiring.*

# 2. THE BRANCHES OVERHANG THE FENCE

### MEDITATION

How good it is to sit in the midst of the congregation—each with his private thoughts and desires, mingling these in one muted chorus with the private thoughts and desires of others whom we touch and see. All this we do without the prying eye and the curious stare. All this we expose to the mind, to the heart, to the love of God. We think of the sick of body and mind, those whose names we call in the quietness, and of numberless others whose misery may be known only to God. We think of men across the sea, symbols for power and place, whose decisions may determine for the rest of us long nightmares of anguish or stretches of tranquillity beneath the friendly sky. We think of ourselves, the loneliness of our own struggles: the sins of our lives; the limitations, the weaknesses; the mounting hopes, the hills of joy from which we see so far; our families, our children, our friends, our enemies.

O God, God, our Father, we have no words, no words by which we dare express the things that stir within us. We lay bare ourselves, our world, before Thee in the quietness. Brood over our spirits with Thy great tenderness and understanding and judgment, so that each of us will find, in some strange new way, strength for our weakness, health for our illness, guidance for our journey. This is the stirring of our hearts, O God, our Father.

### READING

We are in varied ways concerned about welfare and well-being—our own and others'. Rare indeed is the man who looks at his own life, who examines his personal position, and is assured that he is in no need of improvement. The place where a man stands is never quite the place that marks the limit of his powers and the resting point for all his dreams. This is the way of life.

Often it is easier to be concerned about the welfare and well-being of the world, of society, than about our own. Few there be who can escape the urge to join in the general chorus of the age that we have fallen upon evil days. There seems to be a strange weary comfort in taking one's place against the wailing wall. There is a searching danger ever present in all concern, whether personal or social—the concern can, oh so easily, become a substitute for thoughtful planning and action. We are constantly in jeopardy by this possibility. Have you ever said with real feeling, "I must do something about drinking so much coffee" or "I am alarmed over the fact that I can't seem to get down to business with my own personal life"? Of the great number of people who feel outraged over what seems to be a terrible miscarriage of justice, how many do something concrete about it? All the energy is exhausted in such remarks: "How awful"; "What a tragedy"; "Something ought to be done"; "Terrible, what a shame."

Again, our emotional reaction to situations causes us to adopt measures that bring quick and temporary relief so as to relieve the immediate pressures on us but not to have much effect on the situations themselves. The real purpose is to relieve only ourselves. Somehow we must find that which is big enough to absorb us from artificial and ineffective methods to increase welfare and well-being. This means the large view, the great faith, which will release in us the vast courage capable of sustaining us in the long pull toward a valid increase in welfare and well-being. It is for this reason that a religious faith about life and its meaning becomes a necessity for all who would work for a new heaven and a new earth without which there can be no final health either for the individual or the society.

———◆———

The phrase of my subject is taken from the book of Genesis, from the picture of a dying patriarch. These words are those he selected to describe his estimate of his son Joseph. The full text is this: "And thou, Joseph, art a fruitful tree, a fruitful tree by a well of water, whose branches hang over the fence." The tree has grown so large that the fence cannot contain it, and the fruit spills over to the outside. Anybody who is hungry may eat, with or without permission, with or without recognition of the ownership of the tree. A tree so full of fruit that no wall can contain it! It spills over.

We are utterly dependent upon one another. We are the heirs of social experience, even for the very words we use.

The very words he uses, are they ever his?
Through countless years of use and misuse,
Through searching experience deep and wide,
His words now familiar in their setting,
Have gathered into themselves the marks of
Many minds and many climes.
A man's words are never his, alone.
How can he ever say, I, I speak!
The thoughts that pour forth from a mind alive
Are products, cumulative units,
Adopted, appropriated, borrowed, stolen,
Garnered from a thousand fields of mental groping.
A man can never say, "This thought is mine,
And mine alone."
By heroic effort, by subtle transmission, man
Establishes equity in thoughts.
They are never his and his alone.

We are dependent upon one another for the food we eat, the clothes we wear. The sense of dependence is evident everywhere. I think it is rooted in something more profound than a mere awareness of individual lack. I think it is rooted in a need that is fundamental to the human spirit. We cannot survive in isolation. We cannot abide being cut off. We cannot even abide the sense of being cut off. When the individual feels that his rejection is complete and absolute, and that he is a prisoner in his own little private world, with no windows, what happens? Sometimes he begins to hear sounds in the atmosphere, voices that become words communicating ideas. The human spirit in its prison is trying to break out because it cannot survive in isolation.

This profound sense of the necessity for involvement with others moves everywhere through the corridors of human experience, from the life of the individual to the life of the state.

This is why no exclusive alliance among nations can ever survive. Over and over again, in the history of Western civilization, there has been the delusion that if we can organize a group of nations around a single commitment, which does not involve certain other nations, somehow we shall be able to accomplish our declared purpose. But, over and over again, such an alliance collapses. There is nothing in the history of the race that should lead us to think that contemporary alliances will not collapse in the same way. Why? Because they are against life, and if they are against life, they cannot possibly survive. Life means involvement that approaches nearer and nearer to totality and completeness. Any isolation ultimately collapses under the relentless pressure that comes up out of the ground of our being for totality of involvement.

Now we may do various things with this necessity. We may choose to ignore it. In that case, we find ourselves in a very searching personal dilemma. We want to be ourselves, to be independent, to be free of any necessity for involvement, in order that we may have a chance to grow, to become, to fulfill ourselves. Yet there is a pulling all the time in the other direction. When we find a person who deliberately sets out to make his life revolve only around himself, we say he is selfish. A friend of mine took a trip around the world. He had many photographs taken and the phrase he used in showing them was always the same. "Here I am, standing in front of the sphinx. Here I am, in front of Westminster Abbey. Here I am. . . . Here I am. . . ." Well, he was there, of course. I am reminded of the allegory of the ants that spent many, many years building an ant memorial. At last it was complete except for one little spot, one little crevice that needed one grain of sand. When that grain of sand was finally placed, this thing that they had been working on for so long would be finished. And so it happened that in the

line of duty one little ant came carrying a grain of sand; he put
this one grain of sand into one little unoccupied spot. Suddenly
he realized that the work was all done and he looked around
saying, "My, my, look at what I have done! Look at the ant heap
that I have built. My anthill! My world!" Then a wind stirred
down in the valley, swept up over the top of the heap, and car-
ried the vaunting ant to destruction. But the ant mound remained.

Jesus talked about this sense of individual importance. A man
walked around in his field one day and saw that he had more
produce than he could possibly use. He didn't say, "I will share
it with others." He said, "I will tear down my barns, build bigger
ones, and say to my soul, 'Eat, enjoy yourself and grow fat.'"
That night at midnight there was a knock at his door, and
though he could not free himself sufficiently to answer the
knock of the hungry or the destitute, this knock he had to answer. And the voice of death said, "I want you this night." If I
enlarge my area to take in all that I am creating, that it may con-
tinue to be mine, mine, mine, I may even be choked to death
by my own surplus.

Now there is another way to deal with our need for fulfillment. We may more and more identify ourselves with others
until the basic sense of involvement that is a part of the very
nature of life itself becomes an integral part of our consciousness. When this happens, the energy of life itself becomes available to us at the point of our most insistent demand.

I remember talking with Miriam Slade, the English woman
who became a follower of Mahatma Gandhi. She had left her
family in England, all her security, all her friends, to join
Gandhi's ashram. She told me that she had arrived in India
with one little packing case full of the things that she was sure
she needed, just the barest necessities, those things that seemed

to her one with the expression of her personality. At the end of two weeks she sent a bundle back home. At the end of the next few weeks she sent another. She was sending bundles back home for two years because, as more and more she became involved in the life about her, she found, as men over and over again, that the fruit must hang over the fence if the tree is going to live. I must work at the enlargement of my garden, the trees in my garden, keeping them supplied with whatever makes them grow, not only that somebody else may get the fruit, but that my tree itself may be the kind of tree that delights the God of Life. If I do that, I feed the hungry. If the hungry do not know about my tree, I will find the hungry and say to them, "Here, take, eat, and live, and do not thank me; thank the God of Life."

"Thou, Joseph, art a fruitful tree, a fruitful tree by a well of water, whose branches hang over the fence."

————◆————

Be in the fleeting word, our Father, the stumbling effort. Touch mind and heart and life, that as we move from this place into the way that we must take, we shall not be alone, but shall feel Thy Presence beside us, all the way.

# 3. HIGH PRIEST OF TRUTH

We gather together in mind and in spirit, centering our thoughts upon the deepest needs of our personal lives. The week that has passed has been for some of us difficult, hard; for some easy, soft. There are open doors before which we stood but through which we did not enter because we were afraid, because we had too much distraction, because we were too self-confident and complacent, or because we were too busy doing good.

There were temptations to which we yielded, and in the yielding we discovered some things about ourselves that we did not know before. Had anyone asked us two weeks ago, three weeks ago, a month ago, we would have been sure that we would not succumb to a temptation of that kind; but we did, this week that is past. And now there crowd around us ghosts of lost battles.

It is with relief that we feel one another's presence and draw upon one another's strength with the great hope that what we need for ourselves we shall find in the quietness of this hour. And thus—

Our Father, we lay bare our lives to Thee without the dishonesty that marks so much of our daily path; with simplicity of heart and directness of spirit, we hide nothing from Thy scrutiny. The good, the bad, our failures, our successes, our dreams, our desires, we place before Thee in the quietness of this hour.

Brood over us, our God who loves us, until at last we shall be one, whole, healed, lifted, that we may face what awaits beyond this hour with new hope and new courage. For us this is enough. O God, our Father! Amen.

### READING

All this prosperity, as the mere fruit of my toil, has been less easy than for many. I may not boast with the apostle that I have fought a good fight, but I can say that I have fought a hard one. The fight will always be hard for any man who undertakes to conquer life with the few and simple weapons I have used and who will accept victory only upon such terms as I have demanded. For be my success small or great, it has been won without willful wrong of a single human being and without inner compromise or other form of self-abasement. No man can look me in the eyes and say I ever wronged him for my own profit; none may charge that I have smiled on him in order to use him, or called him my friend that I might make him do for me the work of a servant.

*Do not imagine I fail to realize that I have added my full share to the general evil of the world: in part unconsciously, in part against my conscious will. It is the knowledge of this influence of imperfection forever flowing from myself to all others that has taught me charity with all the wrongs that flow from others toward me. As I have clung to myself despite the evil, so I have clung to the world despite all the evil that is in the world. To lose faith in men, not in humanity; to see justice go down and not believe in the triumph of injustice; for every wrong that you weakly deal another or another deals you to love more and more the fairness and beauty of what is right; and so to turn with ever-increasing love from the imperfection that is in us all to the Perfection that is above us all—the perfection that is God.*

—JAMES LANE ALLEN

It is very difficult to talk about the idea of truth without yielding to the temptation to stretch one's self out of shape by trying to become profound. I should like you to think very simply about what I call high priests of truth! Here I use the term "high priest" not in an ecclesiastical sense but to denote a servant; and "truth" as that which makes for wholeness, for integration, for inner togetherness, for a sense of being present and accounted for in one's life.

One way to accomplish this wholeness of life is to make our *talents* high priests of truth. How subtle is the temptation for human beings to take all the credit for their own talents. And how extraordinary that it should be so! A talent is a gift of God. It isn't mine. There is always the gratuitous element in a talent. Of course, I must work at its use, I must develop it; but the talent itself is a gift. I am only the trustee.

Suppose your talent is a good, clear mind, enabling you to understand quickly; you grasp immediately what others toil over. Then one day you wake up to discover that you are surrounded by a lot of very stupid people. You hadn't realized before how dull they are. Now, obviously, this talent is a weapon in your hands. You may find yourself driving the more stupid people into corners. You do not mean to do it, but you can't seem to help it; when your mind starts working, it just *starts working.* But what happens to the other person? There is nothing more merciless and perhaps more disintegrating for personality than to be driven into a mental corner. Your mind appears to be consciously directed toward undermining another's self-confidence.

Question yourself: If you are blessed with a good mind, how do you use it? Do you "throw your weight around" with it? Do not be too quick to say: "That does not apply to me." You can let your good mind be your high priest of truth. Let it work on behalf of the wholeness, the healing, and the integrating of life. Let your mind, your talent, reverence the individuality of others, that less strong minds, less gifted minds, may seek refuge under the shadow of your wings. Simple, isn't it?

Or perhaps your talent is your good looks. Some people are good to look at; and they know it, so they are always showing themselves off, asking innocent questions that encourage people to compliment them, making innocent remarks that seem to imply that they think themselves *not* good looking. But your beauty is a gift of God. You did nothing that guaranteed it, but you have it. It was given to you. Let your beauty be your high priest of truth, making always for wholeness, for healing, for integration. Then, in the shaft of light that your beauty casts, even the most homely person will discover in himself or herself something that is blessed by your touch.

Again, your talent may be one for making friends easily. People are attracted to you. Your subtle temptation is to exploit your success with people and in using it for personal ends, you are likely to develop a profound contempt for your fellows. You find them gullible; they can be taken in easily; they can be fooled, can be wrapped around your finger. You are using this gift of God to write your resignation from the human race because you have put yourself over against others.

But, if you have this gift, this warmth of personality that makes for harmony with others and gives them a sense of reassurance, suppose you let it become a high priest of truth. You will be on the side of the shy person, the one who is deeply inhibited and ingrown, who does not have quite the confidence that is needful for unfolding and making easy contacts with people. Suppose you let this talent of yours shine on those whom you meet until they are warmed clear through. Now they begin to unfold and to blossom, to expand, to make discoveries about their own possibilities, unknown before because they were cold and lonely in their inward parts. When they meet you, when they come into touch with this gift of yours, they will begin to live, thoroughly. For the bruised reed you would not crush, nor the smoking flax you would not put out.

Finally, we should make our advantages, our accidents or incidents of good fortune, high priests of truth! We are born into certain situations. It may happen that the circumstances of birth, our background, our family, gave us the edge over those not so well-placed. But these advantages we did not create. They are essentially unearned increment!

You, for instance, do not have to be hungry. You can, on a cold day, sit in a warm room and wear warm clothes, and have no deep, justifiable fear of tonight or tomorrow. Another warm room awaits you when you leave this room, and clean sheets and nourishing food as well. While, at this moment, millions of people, in bitter weather with no warm room anywhere, with nothing in their experience that holds out hope of change, know that tomorrow will be as today is with little food, little shelter.

An advantage. Yes! Shall it make us arrogant, proud, conceited? Shall we say, as a people, "If you do not think as I think, I will not give you my bread to eat; if you do not believe as I believe, I will not give you clothes to wear"? On what meat do we feed, that we have grown so bold as to think that we merit the advantages that are ours? Unless we are able somehow to make of our worldly advantages high priests of truth (thinking of truth as that which makes for wholeness, for integration, for health), then we virtually announce that life made a mistake in so favoring us. If we acknowledge our gifts, then we undertake to say to life: "Give me time and I will grow up to the faith that you expressed in me when you so blessed my life."

Let each one of us say to himself: "I will make of my talents, I will make of my advantages, I will make of my life itself, a high priest of truth! In the living of my life I shall always keep the real under the close scrutiny of the ideal so that there shall come a time when the ideal shall actually become the real." This is a man's assignment in life. If we betray life, may God have mercy on our souls!

———◆———

*Give us, our Father, the strength and the wisdom without which our souls would sicken and die. Grant that Thy peace may walk with us. Guide us into those paths of which, with Thy whole self, Thou canst approve. Amen.*

# 4. THE GIFT OF MEMORY

## MEDITATION

*How terrifying our individual lives would be if there were no privacy of thought and feeling! Shut up within ourselves, we live a life alone, in a private world which can scarcely be invaded, and it is well. There are moments, however, when we wish to break the seal, to open ourselves that the privacy of our struggle can somehow be shared and the awfulness of our isolation be entered into by someone else, so that our isolation be no longer isolation.*

*This feeling, this desire, this urgency, we recognize both for what it is in terms of our life together with others and as something more—some deep stirring within that calls for something that is deep without. When that which is deep within touches somehow that which is deepest without, a strange sense of se-*

curity comes to us and the well-being which we have sought is at last realized.

Thus, our Father, we pray not with good words nor with bad words, not because we are good people nor bad people; but we pray to Thee because we must, and in that compulsion, we discover Thy love; and we thank Thee, our Father, we thank Thee. This is enough for our spirits. Amen.

### READING

The puppy was blind when he came into the world. His nose meant everything to him. He was always sniffing, and sniffing, and feeling. Perhaps he heard a little also, but his sense of smell was his great gift, the gateway by which he approached the rest of the world. This faculty brought him so much, how could he ever suspect that there was anything that could bring him more? Then at last—oh, amazement! His eyes opened, and he came into a whole world of light. O little dog, what a revelation! What a turning upside down of all your small nose-world! Did you ever dream that this universe was waiting for you? Yet perhaps you had to give those first few sniffing days to training your sense of smell, which all your life will stand you in such good stead. Would you ever have bothered about it had you known what other greater faculty was soon to be yours? If you had had eyes from the very first, would you have troubled to educate your nose? And yet without it how could you ever have had such a rounded life?

—JANE STEGER

---

Store up treasures for yourselves in heaven, where neither moth

nor rust corrode, where thieves do
not break in and steal.

Matthew 6:20

The September, 1954, issue of *Scientific American* was devoted to a discussion of many of the developments of modern science and their bearing upon contemporary life and upon human destiny. One of the most exciting articles in this magazine —perhaps I say it was exciting because it was the only one that I could understand—was a discussion of the meaning of memory; what is memory?

The scientist has some rather interesting things to say and I commend the article to you if you wish to study in capsule form some of the things that are being said about the mechanism of memory. Such a discussion is not a part of my function nor a part of my competency.

If I were to use a text for what I wish to say on the subject, it would be, "Store up treasures for yourselves in heaven, where neither moth nor rust corrode, where thieves do not break in and steal." I would not interpret it in terms that would perhaps conform to the pattern of New Testament study or criticism, but rather would I apply it to the significance of memory in human life and human experience.

Suppose you could not remember. Have you ever thought about it? It would mean that every act of your life would have to be done initially every time. You would have to learn how to walk every time you started to walk; you would have to learn how to breathe every time you started breathing, and what would happen in the interval? If I could not remember, it would mean that I could not learn, that I would be the prisoner of the event. Think of it—the prisoner of the moment, with knowledge of nothing that is previous, nothing that could conceivably antedate the moment. All I would have at any particular time would be the moment, the event. How terrifying that would be!

It was one of the Greek philosophers who said that all learning, all education for that matter, is recollection, and I am sure that there are many students who during examinations believe that. They find that they are not very good Greeks. This philosopher also says that long before man was born the individual soul was born and the soul lived as a soul in the presence of God, exposed to all the truth, to all the beauty, to all the goodness of God. When its time came to be born into the body, it brought into its experience all the memory of this exposure, and its learning was merely recollecting, remembering, recalling.

Now I have two suggestions to make about memory as a gift. The first is a warning that unless we are very careful, we will use our memory—and memory is a tool in my thinking—to store up things that will give us trouble in the future. It is very interesting to notice how we can slip into the mood of remembering all the slights, all the hurts, all the little ways by which individuals tried to make life difficult for us. We store them up and introduce into the experience of memory the *principle of negative discrimination*. By and by, when we have accumulated a store of memories of that sort concerning a particular person, if we see that person coming, we go into action! We call to mind our accumulated store of incidents. We cannot get to that person and that person cannot get to us in this new moment, in this new facing of each other, in this new experience, in this new exposure; the great mountain of cumulated incidents, words, phrases, actions, that have finally so filled our memory have spilled over into all the other areas of our thinking. Our attitude toward life itself gets its clue from our attitude toward this individual life with reference to whom we have accumulated this store of negative memories. Our life becomes negative, pessimistic, suspicious, profoundly mistrusting; we have introduced into our memory pattern a principle of negative discrimination.

The alternative suggestion is that we plan to introduce into our memory pattern, the *principle of excellence*. It is quite possible to go through our days on the hunt for the good things in people, sniffing around to find the worthful thing, the meaningful thing, the positive thing. That is not being a Pollyanna; it is not saying that the negative thing is not there; but what we are now looking at is the totality of the other person—all the negative, the positive, the good, and the bad. We are all mixed; nobody is bad, nobody is good, we are just ourselves.

When I look at you, I have a choice. I can pick out the things in you which, as I look at you, make me ashamed for you. Or I can, as I look at you, exercise another option. I do not say that the negative thing is not there, but I let the principle of excellence, the positive discrimination, lift out from my storehouse the things about you that make me glad that you are alive, and glad that somehow, in the circling movement of the process of life, you and I met. Then, when I see you coming, I can hardly wait to be with you because, as I go through my card index, there appear all the things which rejoice the heart and make me glad that it is possible for human beings to be so good, or so kind, or so gracious as I have discovered you to be. Therefore, in my moments of most ungraciousness, in my moments of most resentment, in my moments that are most negative, I remember you and that memory will, in a sense, create a kind of vacuum that pulls me up to be a better man because I know you. That is laying up for myself treasures in heaven. Nothing can take them away from me.

There are times when life does seem to be out of joint for a lot of reasons. There is a little thing that I do then with my memory—and you will pardon the personal reference here—when all my lights seem to be going out and someone else seems to have his hands on the switch. This one thing I do that no one can control; no one can get to it to do anything with it: I take a piece of paper; on it I make a list of many of the beautiful things that I have seen. It is curious how one beautiful thing reminds me of another and another that had temporarily been covered over. There are the breathlessly wonderful moments that I have had with other human beings, the moments when my mind has been lifted because of the majesty and the strength and the vitality of some inspired word. I make a list of these. By the time I am through, my pump has been primed and the water starts flowing again. I commend it to you! Try it sometime! Try to remember some excellent thing that has come into your life; and the dynamic that was yours when you had the initial experience will be reactivated. Even though it happened twenty-five years ago, it can be stirred to bless today as it blessed then.

It is small wonder that Carlyle suggests, "It was always a serious thing to live," and I recommend to you that you do not show your gratitude to God for His gifts by introducing into your memory a negative principle, but that you rejoice His heart and delight His Spirit by introducing there a principle of excellence. This no one can take away from you, though the winds blow and though the earth be lifted up and turned over; and though the mountains be removed from their place and all of life falls apart. As long as you are you, this can be your priceless treasure. Store it up against a time of famine which is bound to come.

"Store up treasures for yourselves in heaven, . . . where thieves do not break in and steal."

We do not know how to offer our thanksgiving, our Father, in words that match the depth of our feeling and our thought. Accept the mood which Thou hast inspired in us as our offering, yea as our thankful offering.

# 5. HORN OF THE WILD OXEN

## MEDITATION

As we sit together in the quietness, may we lay bare before God the prides of our lives: the pride of family, of name and all the circling series of conceits that nourish it and keep it alive; pride of achievement and all the blindness which urges us to take complete and full credit for that which can never be ours and ours alone; pride of beauty of face, of body, of apparel and decoration; pride of knowledge, as if our little minds could contain the vastness of the regions of wisdom and disciplines to which we are heirs; pride of our goodness with all the smugness that makes us feel that our characters are superior to other characters, that we are better in deed than another; pride of nation that fails us with the harsh discords of vaunting nationalism; pride, pride, pride, arrogance, conceit.

O God, our Father, we make to Thee the offering of our prides. Hold them in Thy hand until none is left to bedevil our days and trample our souls. This is our prayer, O God, who loves us and trusts us, even our Father.

### READING

*I will not be daunted*
*By an interval.*

To experience physical pain and/or its equivalent is to suffer. In suffering, thus defined, there is always a margin of freedom for the movement of the mind and the emotions away from the core of the suffering. It is for this reason that many people who suffer find their creativity intensified, their powers greatly enhanced.

To experience personal despair due to some weakness in one's own character is tragedy. In tragedy, thus defined, the individual stands on the brink of fulfillment, comes within reach of the city of his dreams; something happens, something goes wrong, there is the crucial moment and the precise ingredient needed is not there.

To experience the sense of utter isolation, to feel one's self cut off from all resources, left to one's self, to one's self alone, is to be afflicted. In affliction, thus defined, the individual seems to himself to be deserted not merely by man but by God. It is this last that grips the soul with a frozen agony in which the last iota of energy is consumed by an anguished cry.

Much of the drama of the week of the Passion as observed by the Christian world has to do with the experience of the central Figure of our faith with suffering, the sense of tragedy, and the intense convulsion of affliction. The pain of the cross and the wrenching of the mind and spirit from its intensity; the heavy cry that the cup might pass, when his whole life was threatened with tragedy; the desolation that forced from blistered lips the ancient whimper of the psalmist, "My God, My God, why hast Thou forsaken me"—these were the forms that the drama took.

But deep within the center of the turbulent sequences there stirred something else in response to an insistence in Jesus that moved into him straight from the Heart of God. The words of the opening quotation find their meaning now—

> I will not be daunted
> By an interval.

The power that enables a person to resist the terrible necessity for scaling down his faith, his hopes, his dreams, his commitment, to the level of the event which is his immediate experience, this is finally the meaning of the triumph of life over death, of strength over weakness, of joy over sorrow, of love over hate. This is the power of the resurrection, which is rooted in the life of God, available to all men in every age, in every faith, everywhere.

———◆———

> From the horns of the wild oxen I cried unto Him,
> And He answered me.

We are all involved in what has been aptly called "the tragic fact of life." Soon or late, and sometimes soon and late, we are visited by the tragic fact. What do you do with your tragic fact? Not what can you do with it or what may you do with it, but what do you do with it?

As we look at our suffering or at the sufferings of others, we are struck by the fact that so much of human suffering follows the ordinary logic of events—reaping and sowing. That the two belong together has been deeply imbedded in our minds. I remember that when I was a boy, I broke one or two of the little bones in the right wrist. While my arm was in splints and I couldn't play baseball or go fishing, I amused myself by trying to remember what it was I had done that had merited that discomfort, that pain. I knew that I must have done some very wicked thing, but all the things of which I was capable didn't seem to me to deserve that kind of suffering. This is the way in which we think about our unhappy experiences—antecedent, consequence; reaping, sowing—always on the hunt for the logic of the event. The psalmist in my text refers to the dilemma of the tragic fact as being "on the horns of the wild oxen."

What do you do with your tragic fact? It seems as if the things happening to you are so terrible that in your moments of wildest hostility you would not pass those events on into the life of your worst enemy. There is something about such suffering that seems to be degrading, that seems to insult the human spirit. There is something about it that is unclean and demoniac.

I would make three simple observations. They cannot be regarded as complete answers to the problem of suffering; but they give witness and testimony to my own thinking and feeling.

The first is this: The tragic fact must be placed in some kind of causal context. One of the most disturbing things about the tragic fact that invades my life is that it does not take into account my private concerns. And yet there must be a cause for this thing. For instance, suppose I am wrestling with a disease and because I am thus afflicted, one by one my duties must be neglected, one by one my lights go out. Many of the dreams of my life that were contingent upon robust health must now be abandoned. It seems that I am being dealt with in a manner that is ruthless because it ignores my private world of concerns, ambitions, hopes, and desires. In my desperation, I personalize my tragic fact and am like a little boy who stubs his toe on a root that protrudes from the ground, turns around and kicks the root, hurting his foot all over again, as if the root knew he was coming along and purposely protruded in order to trip him. We tend to pull our tragic fact out of any context whatsoever and treat it as the active agent of a demoniac personal enemy.

So then the first thing I must do with my tragic fact is to put it in a causal context. There is a logic in the disease—not a logic in the disease in relation to me. No, but a logic in the disease itself. For instance, why are we convinced that we can do something about cancer? All the work, all the research that is being done in this area assumes that there is inherent in cancer, in this malignancy, an order, a structure of dependability, a logic. If the rational principle of this disease can be comprehended by the rational principle in my mind, I may be able either to reduce the disease to a manageable unit or to create a specific that will neutralize its effect. My mental process does not immediately cure me of the disease, but it does enable me to recognize that it is not an irrationality in the grip of which I am completely paralyzed. It does not then undermine my confidence in the rational grounding of the universe.

The second thing to do with my tragic fact is to learn when to carry it and when to put it down. That is very difficult. I had a conversation about prayer with a lady whom I met on the train. She asked if I believed in prayer. I said, "Yes, I do." She said, "I do, too. Before I left home this morning, I had my prayer time; and do you know what I did? I took all of my troubles, did them up in one bundle"—here she took about twenty-five minutes' detour to tell me about these troubles—"tied them neatly, and handed them to God. But before He could get the bundle opened, I snatched it back again. I didn't want to trust Him with it." I must carry my burden but I must also be able to put it down. I must not let my tragic fact become the total, thoroughgoing preoccupation of my mind, my energies, and my enthusiasm. If I do, it chokes to death all of the margins that could give me the momentary release, detachment from the intensity of my involvement. Part of the discipline of life is in learning how to put things down and do something else, and then when necessary, to pick them up again. There is nothing new in this idea. But it reminds us that if we become obsessed with the tragic fact, we become the tragic fact. And then we are destroyed by it.

There is a third thing that I must do. I must recognize that in our kind of world much that we think cannot be borne, must be borne anyway. My tragic fact, because of its perennial dynamics, its power, its changeless character, seems to me infinite in its energies. Therefore, I must somehow learn how to put at the disposal of the limitless demands of my tragic fact the boundless resources of God. Instead of enduring it, I can float it.

I must be surer of God than I am of my tragic fact. Now my life becomes a channel through which the energies of God are focused upon my inescapable threat. I discover that what I knew I could not possibly endure, I will endure. From the horns of the wild oxen I cried unto Him, not in panic, not in fear, but with courage and confidence. And He answered me. He answered me!

————◆————

*Give to Thy children Thy Spirit, our Father, as we separate one from the other to take up our own tragic facts.*

# 6. THE GROWING EDGE

*We come together and sit in the quietness, each one of us with his private world, his needs and desires, hopes and fears, troubles and delights. We finger these, one by one, as if by some curious magic each of us is alone, as if he alone existed in all the universe. As we lay bare our private lives, we slowly become aware of another Presence brooding over us. What seems at first merely to be reverie about ourselves and our private lives becomes now a sense of sharing our innermost selves with Another. This we do with the great desperate hope that here at last we may be understood, that we may be given some dimension of mind and spirit that will gather into itself all our lives and give them a meaning, a significance, an overtone, which was not ours before we came. Thus there is born in us new hope,*

174

that we may leave this place lifted up and strengthened. We turn, O God, consciously to Thee, seeking nothing, but exposing ourselves to Thy scrutiny, to Thy love, and to Thy wisdom. Breathe through our needs, O God, our Father, that even our anxieties and distresses of body and mind may become instruments in Thy hands, working in us Thy perfect work. This, O God, our Father, is all our spirits can abide. We do this with quiet confidence. O God, God, our Father.

READING

## AFTER SUNSET

I have an understanding with the hills
At evening when the slanted radiance fills
Their hollows, and the great winds let them be,
And they are quiet and look down at me.
Oh, then I see the patience in their eyes
Out of the centuries that made them wise.
They lend me hoarded memory and I learn
Their thoughts of granite and their whims of fern,
And why a dream of forests must endure
Though every tree be slain: and how the pure
Invisible beauty has a word so brief,
A flower can say it or a shaken leaf,
But few may ever snare it in a song,
Though for the quest a life is not too long.
When the blue hills grow tender, when they pull
The twilight close with gesture beautiful,
And shadows are their garments, and the air
Deepens, and the wild veery is at prayer,
Their arms strong around me; and I know
That somehow I shall follow when you go

175

*To the still land beyond the evening star,*
*Where everlasting hills and valleys are,*
*And silence may not hurt us any more,*
*And terror shall be past, and grief, and war.*
— GRACE HAZARD CONKLING

---

For there is hope of a tree,
    if it be cut down,
that it will sprout again,
and that the tender branch thereof
    will not cease.
Though the root thereof
    wax old in the earth,
and the stock thereof
    die in the ground;
Yet through the scent of water
    it will bud,
and bring forth boughs
    like a plant.
— Job 14:7–9

Brooding over all of life is a Presence that no single event or experience can possibly exhaust. This truth is not peculiar to any one religion but is shared by many; and it is through religion that this universal insight may be made available to the believer.

In the Christian faith great wisdom places the central moment of high celebration to coincide with the coming of spring —the creative season when new life abounds on every hand.

After the crucifixion one of the disciples said, "Well, I'm going fishing." The event outside the city wall seemed to have exhausted the possibility of life and of God, to have made of him who died on the cross its prisoner. Later these disciples had another kind of experience that completely changed their feelings. (Whether or not the Biblical description of what happened commends itself to the modern mind is not basic to the experience.) They now felt that he who died on the cross was not the prisoner of the event of the cross. That is all. I suggest that theirs was an example of a universally valid insight.

There is inherent in the nature of life what I call "the growing edge." We see it in nature; always vitality seems to be nestling deep within the heart of a dying plant. A kind of oak tree comes to mind. You have seen it. The leaves turn yellow and die, but they stay on the tree all winter. The wind, the storm, the sleet, the snow—nothing is able to dislodge these dead leaves from the apparently dead branches. The business of the tree during the long winter is to hold on to these dead leaves. Then there begins to be a stirring deep within the heart of the tree. The expression of its life reverses itself. Its function is no longer that of holding on to the dead leaves. It turns them loose. They fall off. In their places, buds begin to come. What wind, storm, hail, sleet, ice could not do during the long winter, now comes to pass very quietly because of the vitality inherent in the tree. At winter's end people burn the dead grass, so that this growing edge, the vitality inherent in the grass roots, may manifest itself with dignity and with glory.

*No expression of life exhausts life.* The spirit of life broods over every living thing, just as only so long as the spirit of the hive is over the apiary can the bees live and make honey and fulfill themselves. This brooding presence is the aliveness of life.

This same principle expresses itself in human history. During the Black Death, when men were dying like flies and the masses of people were cut off from the sacraments that would have renewed their spirits and given them a sense of security in the presence of death, what happened? There came up, apparently out of the soil of Europe, a group of persons known as the Brethren of the Common Life. They said that the infinite resources of the high God were as close to each person as the beat of his heart. Even though men were cut off from the sacrament, even though there was no altar before which they were permitted to bow, the life of the living God was as close to them as their breathing. Napoleon, in the early nineteenth century, was riding high, standing like some terrifying colossus over Europe threatening to squeeze all of the vitality out of every nation that did not conform to his imperious will. It was a dreadful hour! Many persons awoke each morning feeling that there was no hope for the future. Then what happened? In a log cabin in Kentucky, a baby was born—Abraham Lincoln, whose life was to set in motion a creative process that would undermine all tyrannies. And in England, another baby was born—Charles Darwin, who was to reveal to men the great plan of continuous life on earth; as if, life was saying to life, no experience, no event at any particular moment in time and space, exhausts what life is trying to do. There is always a growing edge.

At the time when the slaves in America were without any excuse for hope and they could see nothing before them but the long interminable cotton rows and the fierce sun and the lash of the overseer, what did they do? They declared that God was not through. They said, "We cannot be prisoners of this event. We must not scale down the horizon of our hopes and our dreams and our yearnings to the level of the event of our lives." So they lived through their tragic moment until at last they came out on the other side, saluting the fulfillment of their hopes and their faith, which had never been imprisoned by the event itself.

In private life, the same thing obtains. You have watched it in the lives of your children or remember it of your own childhood. When you were ten years old, you knew that all the things that happened to you then simply could not exhaust your possibilities. You would have to move into your teens, because then you would be ripe for things that could not be included in your "under ten" dimension. Then, when you were in your teens, you knew that other things were not available to you until you were in your twenties.

> I am a part of all that I have met;
> Yet all experience is an arch wherethro'
> Gleams that untravell'd world, whose margin fades
> For ever and for ever when I move.

So long as you recognize that no event of your life, whatever its character, can imprison you, you will not scale down your aspirations to the level of the facts in your present situation. You will let what rides on the horizon constantly inform the event with which you are wrestling, until at last the event itself begins to open up, to yield, to break down, to disintegrate, under the relentless pressure of some force which transcends the event and tutors and informs it. This is what the Resurrection is all about. Not even death is capable of telling us what it is that God has to say about life. Therefore I will hang on to my event. I will not accept it as the final and ultimate conclusion. I will hold it against all odds until, at last, it disintegrates in my hand because of a quality that is inherent in the very vitality of existence, inherent in the very life of God. I shall not despair. I shall not allow the events of my life to make me their prisoner. I shall believe that life has much more to it than experience disclosed to me. I shall continually believe that God is not through, not merely with life, but with me. I shall co-operate with Him until through my life there begins to pulse something much vaster and greater than anything that I have ever known before. When

I die, I will go down to the grave with a shout, because life is
not through even in death. Life has an infinite creative possibility. This is what Jesus discloses in his trumpet call, "I am
the Resurrection and the Life. He who believes in me will never
die." This is the growing edge.

All around us worlds are dying and new worlds are being born;
All around us life is dying and life is being born.
The fruit ripens on the tree;
The roots are silently at work in the darkness of the earth
Against the time when there shall be new leaves, fresh blossoms,
    green fruit.
Such is the growing edge!
It is the extra breath from the exhausted lung,
The one more thing to try when all else has failed,
The upward reach of life when weariness closes in upon all
    endeavor.
This is the basis of hope in moments of despair,
The incentive to carry on when times are out of joint
And men have lost their reason; the source of confidence
When worlds crash and dreams whiten into ash.
The birth of a child—life's most dramatic answer to death—
This is the Growing Edge incarnate.
    Look well to the growing edge!

———————◆———————

. Turn us not away, O God, from the infinite glory of the commonplace. Be with us and in us, our Father, as we go our separate
ways, and grant that we be not deceived into dependence merely
upon our own minds and our own spirits. Out of Thy long wisdom with Thy children, tutor our spirits, tutor our spirits, O
God, our Father.

# REFERENCES

In addition to the Meditations and Readings written by the author for this book, some of the material is from the following sources:

By the author: Meditation, page 45, and Readings, pages 56, 111, 118, from *Deep Is the Hunger*, Harper, 1951; Meditation, page 21, from *The Greatest of These*, Eucalyptus Press, 1944; Reading, page 22, from *Meditations of the Heart*, Harper, 1953.

*The Hand of God* by Oswald W. S. McCall, Harper, 1939: Readings, pages 8, 47, 87, 125.

*Stories, Dreams and Allegories* by Olive Schreiner, Benn, 1931: Readings, pages 2, 78.

*Wilderness Songs* by Grace H. Conkling, copyright, 1920, by Henry Holt and Company, 1948 by Grace H. Conkling, and used by permission: Reading, page 175.

*Life* magazine, October 10, 1955: Reading, page 15.

*Wings of Healing*, edited by J. Wilmer Gresham, Morgan Press, 1953: Reading by Margaret Cropper, page 31.

"The Hollow Men" from *Collected Poems 1909–1935* by T. S. Eliot, copyright, 1936, by Harcourt, Brace and Company, Inc., and used with their permission and also that of Faber and Faber: Reading, page 102.

*The Boston Daily Globe*, December 9, 1955: Meditation, page 109.

*The Choir Invisible* by James L. Allen, Macmillan, 1898: Reading, page 156.

*Leaves from a Secret Journal* by Jane Steger, Little, Brown, 1926: Reading, page 162.